Keep smiling!

Nancy Lewis

Praise for
SMILING AT STRANGERS

"In these tumultuous, chaotic, and divisive times in which we find ourselves comes a breath of fresh air. Nancy's book is this breath; a powerful yet simple manifesto for all of us. Read this book!! Practicing kindness will change your world."

—Dr. Gloria Harrison, Clinical Psychologist

"In a compact book that flows smoothly, Nancy has captured the spirit of spreading kindness with intentionality. Her personal stories remind us of the small ways in which we can make a big difference in others' lives. Reading her book has had a huge impact on how I go through my days, being more aware of opportunities to be kind and taking action. This is a must-read book for our challenging times."

—Deborah Moskowitz,
Developmental Disability Trainer & Consultant

"As an introvert, I could directly relate to the anecdotes in *Smiling at Strangers*. Unlike many self-help books, it does not purport to improve your career, relationship, or other self-driven goals. Instead it offers a compelling reason to tackle social discomfort: the possibility of making the world a better place one smile at a time."

—Jeremy Jusak, Software Developer

"A self-confessed introvert, author Nancy Lewis shares in her book *Smiling at Strangers* her late-in-life awakening to the power of smiles and connecting with others while simultaneously expanding her own humanity. The book is an antidote to self-preoccupied, individualistic America and fosters a more connected and communal public awareness. Her smiles and philosophy incorporate the best values of religions and humanism. This important work is a response to a growing consciousness that says for humankind to survive, we must globalize kindness and connection. As Nancy says,

'Take your amazing self into the world with a smile and a light heart, and it will be reflected back to you. The world is waiting for you.'"

—Don Duffy, EdD, Emeritus,
University of Central Oklahoma

"Nancy uses her simple story to convey a profound message. Small conscious changes in our lives can have a big effect on us, and on those around us. Her writing delights and inspires, bringing to life the simple steps we can make to bring more joy to the world. Enjoy!"

—Dr. Geoffrey Carr, Psychologist

"With her plea advocating kindness, using everyday anecdotes and quotes, Nancy has really hit it out of the park. As a healthcare professional, father, and introvert, I find many parallels in her journey using kindness as a tool to better connect with other people. This not only helps those people I deal with every day feel at ease with me, but helps me feel better about myself and what I do to help them. Kindness is a win/win endeavor."

—Michael Moorhouse, Healthcare Professional, RN

"A brilliant and marvelous book! Nancy has lovingly and lucidly illuminated an action that can change the world. We need to follow her example."

—Ham Hayes, Owner & Principal Consultant
at Ham Hayes Consulting

"*Smiling at Strangers* offers a simple and much needed strategy for developing connection and healing divisiveness."

—Skye Burn, Principal at Skye Burn Productions LLC

SMILING AT STRANGERS

How One Introvert Discovered the Power of Being Kind

Cover design: Rick Lewis

Print ISBN: 978-1-09832-622-7
eBook ISBN: 978-1-09832-623-4

Printed in the United States of America
www.smilingatstrangers.net

To the kindhearted introverts of the world

It's OK to be scared.

Do it anyway.

Three things in human life are important: the first is to be kind; the second is to be kind; and the third is to be kind.

—Henry James

My religion is kindness.

—H.H. the 14th Dalai Lama

You must do the thing you think you cannot do.

—Eleanor Roosevelt

CONTENTS

A NOTE FROM THE AUTHOR

Welcome, Kind Reader.

Whether or not you're a fellow "introvert," something in you likely knows the world needs more kindness. Especially now, in the Time of the Coronavirus.

When the virus announced its presence on the planet as we moved into a new decade, I was making plans to launch this book in my hometown of Bellingham, Washington, in late spring, and use it to spark a local kindness movement fueled by fellow introverts. Normally, this is the time when Pacific Northwest residents come out of hibernation from the short days and wet gray of winter and begin hitting the streets, shops, parks, and wooded trails, where encounters with strangers are common.

Instead, spring brought with it a global pandemic that restricted our presence in public settings except for purchasing food and other necessary supplies while maintaining six feet of distance, marked with tape on store floors.

So I put a hold on the publication and book launch plans, assuming it wasn't a time to release a book advocating face-to-face connection with strangers.

Then something happened . . .

As I made my forays into food stores to replenish supplies, I noticed that while some people seemed intent on getting in and out with as little interaction with others as possible, some were finding ways to connect and offer kindnesses to strangers. Like the man who noticed I'd left my cloth shopping bags in the bottom of my cart when the checker said they'd been instructed to pack all purchases in paper bags. Allowing kindness to overcome fear, the man followed me out to the parking lot and knocked on the window of my car, holding up the bags so I could lower the window enough to receive them.

While walking through the park that borders my apartment complex, I was surprised at the increase in vocal greetings I got from others as we passed one another (while wearing our masks and maintaining safe social distance). I soon learned that a "hi" or "good morning" and a raised hand communicated a shared acknowledgment of our connection.

Social creatures that we are, and kind at heart, many of us have found ourselves adapting and finding ways to "smile" at each other in creative and joyful ways. As I watched YouTube videos of Italians on their balconies singing together, I was reminded of the Dr. Seuss book *How the Grinch Stole Christmas*. The Grinch stole gifts from the children of Whoville in an attempt to stop Christmas, but the villagers instead stole and enlarged his small heart through the power of love and inclusion as they sang and feasted in celebration of the spirit of Christmas, even without material gifts.

Whether it's singing from our balconies or porches together, organizing drive-by birthday celebrations, meeting neighbors who have been strangers for years as we've been busy engaging ourselves in the outside world, or having Zoom calls with distant friends and relatives, connection is happening.

Perhaps, I thought, this is the perfect time to remind people of what our hearts know. The perfect time to reinforce the message of our essential human need to acknowledge and connect with one another—strangers, friends, and family—through gestures of simple kindness like those my book suggests and illustrates. Although the world in which it was written isn't the one into which it is being birthed, the call to join in creating a kinder and gentler world has never been more urgent.

Let's do this together.

Nancy Lewis

June 2020

PROLOGUE

Smile at strangers and you just might change a life.
—Steve Maraboli

It's a bright early-spring Saturday—downtown farmers market day in Bellingham, the Northwest coastal city where I live. The market is one of my weekly shopping stops April through October. I leave my car in a public parking lot a block away and begin walking toward the market. Along the way I encounter a young mother pushing an infant in a stroller with three other children, two to five years of age, in tow.

Her expression suggests she hasn't had a happy morning at the market.

As I approach the family, I step aside, make eye contact with the harried mother, and simply smile. Her face transforms as she smiles in return, and her soft "Thank you" communicates a degree of gratitude beyond what a simple smile may seem to merit.

This single act is one of the greatest gifts we can give one another. The message it sends is *I see you and acknowledge our kinship as members of the human species doing the best we can. I wish you well.*

Two strangers. A moment of human contact.

I see you.

Every time you smile at someone,
it is an action of love, a gift to that person,
a beautiful thing.
—Mother Teresa

CALLED TO BE KIND

Kindness is the light that dissolves all walls between souls, families, and nations.
—Paramahansa Yogananda

You may or may not consider yourself a fellow introvert, as I refer to myself in the subtitle of this book, but I'm assuming that since you're looking at it, something in you knows the world needs more kindness and is willing to give it. Like me, you're called to be kind. Even if, like me, you're scared.

Yes, people scare me. That's my secret. And I know I'm not alone. A gentle and deeply spiritual man I greatly admire once surprised me by saying the same thing. I remember his exact words: "I'm scared of everybody. I'm even scared of my neighbor's five-year-old daughter." More specifically, the prospect of interacting with others—strangers, and sometimes even friends and family—scares us.

We're called introverts. And we have a lot of company. Estimates suggest that we make up 30 to 50 percent of the population. There's a subgroup of us that psychologists call shy or socially anxious introverts. Hiding is what we do: avoiding people—especially strangers—when we can; taking care of business in as quick and unobtrusive a way as possible when we can't. Being invisible.

Some of us get really good at it. I spent eighty years refining the disappearing skill before I decided there was a more fulfilling way to live. A way to make my life and the lives of the people I encountered happier, at least for a moment, in an increasingly impersonal world. A way to remind people that kindness still lives on the planet.

The decision to do something different was prompted by a sequence of events that occurred three years ago, in the spring of 2017.

The first took place on a crisp April morning when I needed to run some errands and had taken a break from the editing job I was working on (editing being an occupation kind to introverts, unlike the teaching non-career I abandoned after two years in the classroom almost six decades ago).

My first stop was the post office to mail a package and buy some stamps. Next was the library to return the novel I'd just finished reading and pick up another that I'd put on hold. A quick stop at the local market for a few groceries was my final task for the day.

Routine stuff. Get it done; get home. Hit and run.

But this time, something different happened. As I approached the store entrance, I noticed a man sitting slouched against the wall a few feet from the door: indeterminate age, a weathered face partially obscured by a long and scraggly beard, a motley assortment of ill-fitting clothes on a thin body. My gut tightened and my heartbeat ratcheted up a notch as an urge to acknowledge him in some way arose.

As was typical for me at the time, fear prevailed, and I reflexively turned away to avoid making eye contact as I hurried past him and into the store.

While I briskly walked the aisles adding the few things I needed to my grocery cart, my gut continued to churn as my heart and mind carried on a debate.

"Why didn't you stop and ask if he could use a cup of coffee or a sandwich? Or maybe offer him money so he could buy what he wants?"

"Because I'd have to interact with him and I don't know what to say. I even have trouble talking to people I know. What do you say to a street person?"

"Imagine it was one of your sons or grandsons sitting there. Would you be so quick to dismiss him and walk away?"

"I don't even want to think about that. It's too painful."

"But you could at least have made eye contact and acknowledged his existence. Maybe even smiled."

I was only half present as I checked out my purchases, the inner dialogue continuing to absorb my attention. My mind was further occupied anticipating a second walk past the man who was the source of my agitation when I left the store.

But when I walked out, he was gone. There was no sign of him in the parking lot. Nothing to indicate that he'd been there at all.

One more bypassed opportunity to extend a small kindness to people I encounter every day as I go about my business. One more time I'd let fear override my impulse to acknowledge those I share the world with—even if it was only with a smile.

The second event occurred about a week later on a balmy afternoon when I'd paired a walk with a short stop at the same market. As I was leaving the store, I noticed a young man—early to mid-twenties—leaning against the corner of the building nearest the entrance. He didn't look homeless. What he looked was forlorn, watching customers going about their business. He was looking at me as I left the store and began walking in his direction. I could easily have avoided him by altering my route home, but with the previous week's event still fresh in my mind and conscience, I intentionally walked close enough to make eye contact with him, smiled, and said hello. He didn't return my smile or greeting, nor did he look away.

Surprisingly, I didn't feel rejected or embarrassed. It was clear that it wasn't about me. He'd been seen and acknowledged. I was the instrument. It was my first lesson in divesting myself of responsibility for the response—or lack of one—from those I choose to be open to. A genuine smile and a greeting are a gift offered to another. It's not our responsibility if it's not acknowledged—or accepted. This is a hard lesson for us socially shy introverts to learn.

The two supermarket encounters had gotten my attention. The third event, on a walk along a wooded trail that borders the apartment complex where I live, made it clear that it was time to come out of hiding and focus on what I had to offer others instead of on my own perceived inadequacies and fear.

When I walk, I carry a small notebook to catch ideas and musings that often arise. On this occasion I had stopped and stepped to the side of the trail to make a note when I became aware of someone approaching me from behind. A man I guessed to be in his mid-sixties offered a cheery "Hello" as he passed. Startled by his friendly greeting, I responded in kind with an echoing hello.

I finished my note and resumed my walk, the man now about fifty yards ahead of me. The unexpectedness and warmth of his greeting had struck a resonant chord in me. Curiosity overcame my usual reticence to engage a stranger, and I impulsively moved into high gear, overtaking him and matching his pace. He acknowledged my presence with a welcoming smile, as though I were an old friend.

"Excuse me," I said. "Your greeting when you passed me a few minutes ago sounded like you're a happy person. I know it's a personal question, but I'm curious about what your secret is."

His smile grew broader. "Just be kind to people," he said.

The simplicity of his advice belied its significance. "I think you've hit on what might heal the world," I replied.

"One person at a time" were his parting words. We exchanged waves as we went our separate ways into a world awaiting our small contributions to healing a disconnected world.

The spontaneity and assurance with which I'd approached the stranger surprised me. It was the first solid block in building a foundation of confidence in my ability to challenge my reluctance to interact with strangers and offer the small kindnesses I felt were so badly needed in a hurting world.

Once I committed to action, serendipities began occurring: further incidents and interactions that I was able to turn into illustrative anecdotes; ideas and reflections on the nature of being human and the need for connection; quotes about kindness and calls to service.

I continued to surprise myself by the "extrovertiveness" I found myself exhibiting as I began putting this late-life new mission into practice. It seemed so out of character. It wasn't until I read Susan Cain's book *Quiet: The Power of Introverts in a World That Can't Stop Talking* that I learned the secret. Cain's research led her to state that "introverts are capable of acting like extroverts for the sake of work they consider important, people they love, or anything they value highly."

What you're about to read are reflections, ideas, suggestions, and musings on the nature of being human, plus stories from my own quiet life and experience gathered over eight decades on the planet. My hope is that what you find here encourages you to begin your own journey toward making the world you inhabit, large or small, a kinder, gentler place.

Trust me. If I can do it, you can.

A WAITING WORLD

A single act of kindness throws out roots in all directions, and the roots spring up and make new trees.
—Amelia Earhart

The Invitation

We all know it's there: the disconnection and loneliness. Like me, you've sensed it waiting behind the feigned and painful indifference of people taking refuge in their iPads and smartphones: standing at bus stops, in line at the local coffee shop or pharmacy, sitting in waiting rooms, walking the crowded but lonely streets. You've seen it in the faces of people standing on street corners holding hand-lettered cardboard signs that say, "Homeless. Anything helps," or sitting outside supermarkets looking lost, abandoned, and hungry for more than just physical sustenance. A whole world of people waiting to be seen, acknowledged, valued—heard.

Somebody has to be willing to break the trance and remind us that we're all in this crazy world together so we can begin the healing process of seeing and acknowledging one another, even if it's only with a smile.

How about if we do it together?

The Question

I wheel my loaded grocery cart into the checkout lane at one of my favorite Bellingham food markets, expecting the usual light and polite interchange with the checker. But this is no usual checker. It's clear by the way he begins efficiently moving the items across the scanner and by the brightness on his face and in his voice that he's engaged in the world in a way that goes beyond his grocery-clerk job description.

My initial assessment is verified by the first words he speaks.

"Can I ask you a question?" he begins (echoes of my accosting the kind stranger on the trail) before proceeding to describe a hypothetical situation. "Imagine you're a member of an organization called The World-Wide Federation to Evolve the Human Species. As a member of the Federation, you have the opportunity to grant to all humans one characteristic or skill that would help them assist the evolution of the species. What would it be?"

I barely pause before answering. "Compassion," I say.

"That's the most frequent answer I've gotten from all the people I've asked," he tells me.

My first reaction was affirming: a feeling that maybe there was hope for the world after all. Then I remembered a warning from Susan Sontag in a quote I'd recently encountered: *"Compassion is an unstable emotion. It needs to be translated into action, or it withers."*

The Dilemma

I'm out for a neighborhood walk on a soft summer evening shortly after my encounter with the grocery checker who prompted the compassion consideration. As I approach one of the local churches, I notice a young man sitting on the steps of the fellowship hall with his head down and his hands between his legs. He looks up as I draw near, and I smile and say hello. There is no response. Behind him, a man with a briefcase exits the door and walks directly in front of me, striding purposefully toward his car without looking my way or acknowledging the presence of the young man on the steps.

A Christian fellowship hall where fellowship was clearly needed, and none was given. What stories were occupying the minds of these two souls? What answer would they have given had they been offered the hypothetical situation posed by the grocery checker?

This is the world we live in. A world where it's easy to give lip service to the need for kindness, generosity, and the healing balm of compassion, yet we allow the busyness of our lives and our lack of presence in the real world to blind us to everyday opportunities to offer it—even if we're not shy introverts.

I can't in good conscience condemn the man who strode from the church without acknowledging—maybe without even seeing—the dejected young man on the steps. I know his world too well. He was too busy engaging his internal dialogue: perhaps reviewing how he'd screwed up an important meeting; worrying about the pay raise he expected and didn't get; rehearsing the conversation he needs to have with his wife when he gets home.

Compassion for the other requires being present, and if you're like me, most of the time you're simply not there to see what's right in front of you.

What's the nature of the internal dialogue that keeps you from being available and willing to render simple kindnesses when opportunities present themselves? Mine is about how to stay invisible. I hide to avoid being a target for others to judge and reject.

Sharing the Pain of Loneliness

> ***Everyone is screwed up, broken, clingy, and scared, even the people who seem to have it more or less together. They are much more like you than you would believe. So try not to compare your insides to their outsides.***
>
> —Anne Lamott

Although we haven't met, I begin with the assumption that we share Anne Lamott's observation that we're much more alike than we seem. And this goes for both introverts and extroverts. While our personas may differ widely, even the shiniest and brightest versions of what we present to the world are polished for public consumption, while inside we harbor secret doubts and debilitating fears.

This is what it's like for me, and I imagine for many of you who are reading this, even as we put on a good front in public.

Sometimes we're up and happy, feeling connected and expanded beyond our small-me world. Sometimes we feel down and disconnected, inhabiting an inner world of isolation and loneliness.

We struggle between impulses that are fear-based and isolating and those that are love-based and connecting. When fear is dominant and we find ourselves withdrawing and circling our inner wagons against a perceived threat, as the young man on the church steps was perhaps doing, what we really long for is connection and inclusion. Our energy is drained, and we feel sapped and unmotivated, depressed in mind and body. When the love impulse is dominant, our energy is high. We feel glad to be alive and are looking for new worlds to explore. In that state we're filled with joyous confidence that we can do whatever we set our minds to. Our dominant emotion is gratitude, and we feel a call to compassionate action.

I believe that the outer world we inhabit reflects this polarized inner state. It seems the war between love and fear is in full battle mode, and we're on the battlefield, personally and globally, whether we choose to be or not.

I want a fairytale ending where the forces of good overcome the forces of evil, even as I recognize it's not that simple. We humans are far too complex to inhabit fairytales. There are no evil witches and vicious warlords to blame for the situation we find ourselves in, or heroic princes on white horses coming to save the day—and the world. There is just us, imperfect and conflicted as we are.

You and me, together. Kindness power in action.

Too often we underestimate the power of a touch, a smile, a kind word, a listening ear, an honest compliment, or the smallest act of caring, all of which have the potential to turn a life around.

—Leo Buscaglia

WHAT MATTERS

Do your little bit of good where you are; it's those little bits of good put together that overwhelm the world.

—Desmond Tutu

Anytime anyone writes anything, it embodies a set of beliefs and values. Here are mine:

- Something is wounded and hurting—in ourselves, in people we care about, in the human species, in the world at large—and is in need of healing.
- Healing requires thinking and acting in ways that promote kindness and compassion toward one another, including those with whom we disagree.
- Any healing action that benefits one, benefits the whole, as a pebble dropped into a lake causes ripples that extend throughout the entire body of water.

Everything Is Connected

My working hypothesis is that what we do as individuals affects everything. If we behave with kindness, everyone benefits in some measure. If we behave unkindly and without consideration for others, the world in some small or large measure suffers. It's my belief that if there is any hope for this hurting world—the planet and all who share it—those of us who are willing must take responsibility for bringing the healing touch of loving-kindness to those we encounter wherever we find ourselves.

I lead a simple life. My age and occupation as a writer and editor make it easy for me to indulge my naturally introverted nature and habits. I have limited venues in which to make myself available and engage with other people. Most often it's in store aisles and checkout stands, in shared public spaces such as the laundry facility of my apartment complex, and walking along the streets and wooded trails in my neighborhood. Those are places where it's easy to withdraw into a private world and court invisibility. I know this. I've lived it. I also know they're perfect places to practice the connection and engagement that transform *me* into *we*.

Let life unfold like a treasure hunt with clues hidden behind every smile. Greet people with fresh eyes and an open heart like Alice, curious about what they have to offer you and what you have to give them.

—Caitlin Johnstone

FLIPPING THE "M": WHEN ME BECOMES WE

Take a deep breath and tell us your deepest, darkest secret, so we can wipe our brow and know that we're not alone.

—Alan Watts

Deep breath. Here goes . . .

My deepest, darkest secret is the fear that I'm flawed in some crucial way that makes me undeserving of the love and regard of others. I'm missing something essential, and I risk having that revealed every time I interact with other (real) humans, who will then reject me.

Are you still there?

I'm guessing you are. You may even be exhaling a sigh of relief that you're not alone. Unless you've had extraordinarily good luck in your early childhood influences or were born with a naturally sunny and self-accepting personality coated with psychic Teflon, it's unlikely you grew up without any uncertainties about your worth, unscathed by the message that you don't measure up to other people. It seems to be part of our Western cultural heritage with its emphasis on "rugged individualism." *Compete and Win* is the name of the American game.

I've encountered "my" secret in many people I've interacted with over the years, especially in women of my generation: the paralyzing belief that something is fundamentally wrong with us personally and the terror of having it revealed, with the consequence of being judged and abandoned.

As a shy introvert, I've been prey to this belief for most of my life. It's taken eight decades to challenge it, and I'm only willing to do it now because I've convinced myself that connecting with others and offering small kindnesses is more important than indulging my fear of strangers.

What I'm learning in the process is that what I thought was "missing" isn't something in me personally. What's missing is my reluctance to acknowledge that I'm part of a greater whole. Ironically, it is identification with that "greater whole" that's our refuge and hope, both personally and as a member of a global population.

To deny our connectedness makes as much sense as claiming the cells of our body are all separate and can choose to go it alone. When I look at the current state of the shared world we inhabit, what I see is that we're on a sinking life raft, and our fate depends on our willingness to give up the illusion that we can live a separate existence without responsibility to anyone but ourselves. Without acknowledging kinship and relationship, not only with other humans but with all sentient beings, including the living planet we share, we can't survive—as individuals or as a species. It's past time to acknowledge what our gut, if not our head, has known all along: *There is no me without we.*

Considering "the Other"

I believe that nothing is more healing and nurturing than what occurs when two kindhearted strangers let down their guard and meet in a *we* moment with a smile and a simple greeting. I contend that initiating a brief interaction with a stranger, far from being trivial, is one of the most powerful actions we can take in this world that seems to be increasingly fearful of "the other." Such interactions come without the baggage of a story about who this "other" is and what is required of us in response (self-imposed or culturally expected). We're simply two human beings encountering each other in line at the supermarket, post office, or coffee shop; standing at the bus stop; or passing each other on the street or trail. Any interaction, however simple and brief, communicates: *I see you. I acknowledge that you exist.* Coupled with a smile, it conveys the message: *I'm OK, you're OK. I mean you no harm. You can relax in my presence.*

This is what simple looks like.

As I'm trail walking one afternoon, I notice ahead of me a man with two identical-looking small bulldogs, each pulling in a different direction. I stop and watch as the man attempts to keep from getting entangled in their leashes.

"Looks like you've got two hands full," I say.

"Same species, different ages, different personalities," he responds.

"Just like people," I say, as we part and continue on our separate ways.

Further along, I pass a woman with a dog and comment on the pretty color of the dog's fur, adding, "I'd like to have hair that color."

The woman, an age-mate, laughs and says, "I'd like to have hair."

Ripples in the Stream of Life

Remember there's no such thing as a small act of kindness. Every act creates a ripple with no logical end.

—Scott Adams

It's a clear and gorgeous January morning in the Southern California city where my husband Richard and I are spending two weeks in the sun for him to bike and me to work on an editing job. I'm sitting at a table near the pool just starting to work when a young man with a leaf blower and a power mower shows up and begins his grounds maintenance duties.

Choice point: Do I go with annoyance at the interruption of my (clearly more important) work and give him a stony look of reproach as he passes my table? Or do I acknowledge him with a smile and a "Good morning"? Do I engage the "What about me?" question, or allow my body to relax into a "What about we?" consideration?

The choice I made and the brightness of the young man's return smile turned the day even sunnier. Once I decided to expand my universe to encompass *we* instead of making it about *me*, I was able to relax and work even in the presence of the noise of the machinery, marveling at the almost magical way in which energy is released and focused when we acknowledge that we're not the center of the universe. He was doing his job, and I was doing mine. Best of all, every person each of us encountered in the course of our day benefited from the ripples set in motion by my choice to offer a simple smile and greeting and his to respond in kind.

Our "small acts" are small only in how little effort it takes to make them. I choose to put my attention on dropping pebbles of kindness into our shared world pond and trust that the ripples will have large consequences. And I keep in mind that small acts that arise from anger, fear, and other negative emotions have equally large effects that pollute that same world pond.

Are You In?

Writing and publishing this book is an act of faith that something good will come of it. I hope you're still with me. I can make a difference, but I can't change the world alone.

> ***I alone cannot change the world, but I can cast a stone across the waters to create many ripples.***
>
> —Mother Teresa

THE LOVE CONNECTION

Fear and hatred will cease to exist
when love is in abundance.
—Ken Nwadike Jr

The Wounded Heart

In 1976, two decades into my marriage to Richard, we moved from Milwaukee, Wisconsin, where Richard had been teaching at a women's college, to Arkansas, where he'd taken a job at the University of Arkansas at Little Rock. We had lived in Milwaukee for nine years, the longest period of time we had stayed anywhere, and the first place I'd begun to grow roots and develop a sense of belonging and community. Leaving friends behind and beginning again terrified the scared and introverted little girl who shared my forty-year-old body. Although the move made perfect sense in regard to Richard's career, it was emotionally wrenching for me, and I assumed for both of our sons, one in seventh grade and the other in tenth. I hadn't matured enough to handle my own emotions, and I projected them onto my children, taking on the load for the three of us and internally blaming my husband. Us against him. It was the rockiest stage of our marriage.

One of my most vivid memories of that time is of sitting beside Richard in our car in awkward and strained silence after a rare and unusually intense and hurtful exchange that had occurred just before we left the house. Words had been said and misinterpreted, and independent stories had been spun. Facial expressions had become stony, body language rigid and distancing. I don't recall where we were going that day. It's not important. What is important is that my body knew viscerally the intolerable pain of hell. Of separation from the beloved.

After we'd reconnected and I'd had a chance to consider the delicate nature of intimate relationships, even those that are solid and strong at the core, I wrote the following lines:

We are wounded spirits, you and I,

Speaking love in hushed and fragile voices.

It was intended as the beginning of a poem, but it never got completed. I believe it stands alone in describing our human condition. Perhaps we are all to some degree wounded spirits speaking love in hushed and fragile voices, wanting desperately to be heard and seen for who we truly are, to be rescued from the loneliness of going it alone, even as we live ostensibly happy and fulfilled lives.

Somewhere the deepest desire for a soul is to be appreciated, to be loved.

—Jean Vanier

Love Always Rules

What gives me hope is that life unfailingly responds to the advances of love.

—Nipun Mehta

Our fourteen-year-old granddaughter has a T-shirt that says LOVE ALWAYS RULES. It's a potent reminder of what I choose to tell myself is the default position of the human race. We're born with the GIVE AND RECEIVE LOVE setting in the ON position. Unfortunately, that default position appears to get reset in many of us as we encounter a world full of imperfect beings who have come to believe that love is scarce and unreliable and that we're unworthy of it.

I'm not speaking of the fickle form of love that often characterizes romantic love, although romantic love may evolve into it, but of the Great Love that encircles, encompasses, and embraces unconditionally. The love reflected in the saying that home is where you're always welcome, always accepted with open arms, never turned away. The place where the love of unconditional acceptance and inclusion "always rules." The love that provides sanctuary.

How many of us can say we have such a sanctuary? How many of us provide one for others?

For small creatures such as we the vastness is bearable only through love.

—Carl Sagan

The Healthiest Emotion

With all the woes of a world awash in bad news and manufactured drama, it's easy to lose sight of the basic blessing we all share: the capacity for gratitude. For me, a potent reminder came during a Thanksgiving meal with our younger son and his family. My daughter-in-law suggested we each share one thing we were grateful for. When it was his turn, our then twelve-year-old grandson said simply, "Life."

Endocrinologist Hans Selye, who did pioneering work in stress and its effects on the human organism, identified gratitude as the healthiest emotion. Spiritual teacher Arnaud Desjardins, in his book *The Jump into Life: Moving Beyond Fear,* tells us, "Gratitude is the first pure religious feeling." While we may not relate to being "religious," gratitude, to me, implies recognition and acknowledgment that a gift has been freely offered.

How many of us overlook being grateful not only for the big things, like life itself, but for simple kindnesses offered to us by others?

In the moments we are awake to the wonder of simply being alive, gratitude flows, no matter our circumstances.

—M.J. Ryan

Love's Saving Grace

As I begin the day's writing, I'm looking out at two young boys—perhaps eleven or twelve—talking with each other as they push their bikes across the grassy courtyard below my window. They're deeply engaged in whatever young boys converse about when they're out biking together on a sunny summer morning.

I also sense their two intangible companions: friendship and vulnerability. Friendship is obvious. It's bright and vivid in these two young souls just beginning their life journey. Vulnerability is a paler ghost. Yet, in spite of the boys' age and vitality and the protective helmets they wear, vulnerability is the stronger presence.

As full of life as they are in this carefree moment of youth, these two boys will at some point die. And they will leave behind others who deeply grieve their loss. This is what we all live with: the ever-present awareness of our own finiteness, as inconceivable as the thought of ceasing to exist is. Even more painful and terrifying is the awareness that, before our own death, we may suffer the loss of those we love even more deeply than we love ourselves; those we would give our own lives for.

How can we live with such knowledge without compassion? Without kindness to one another in our shared vulnerability?

While I was working on this piece, Richard and I had breakfast with a male friend at a neighborhood café. Our friend had recently returned from a visit to his mother and recounted an altercation they'd had which had cut short his visit. He told us his mother had recently joined a fundamentalist church and was proselytizing him about her newfound faith. She was concerned about the fate of his soul if he didn't accept her church's redemption beliefs. Even worse, her new church preaches that a parent is responsible for a child's salvation and will suffer the pain of eternal separation from the child if they refuse to accept those beliefs. Our friend, an avowed atheist in his late fifties, was angry because his mother wouldn't "listen to reason" and accept his disinterest. Although they'd previously had a close relationship and talked often, he'd decided to distance himself from her rather than put up with further proselytizing.

Richard picked up the conversational ball and shared his own story about having difficulties with his family when he left the church in which he was raised. The conversation continued as the two talked about the frustration of trying to "talk reason" with people who are adherents of fundamentalist faiths.

After listening for a while, I placed my hand on the table and said, "How about trying compassion?" Having gotten the attention of these two intelligent, caring men, I continued. "Imagine the state of terror a mother must be in if she believes her child is damned to hell and eternal separation from her and God if they refuse the salvation story she's placed her faith in."

Our breakfast companion got it. He put his own hand on the table in acknowledgment and said, "She's right! What I need to do is go give my mother a hug!"

Where are we without compassion for one another?

Kindness Elicits Kindness

Deeds of kindness are equal in weight to all the commandments.

—The Talmud

The year before I was born, close to a century ago, a pioneer of the self-improvement movement named Dale Carnegie wrote a classic book called *How to Win Friends and Influence People*. The book is still in print. According to Wikipedia, "One of the core ideas in

[Carnegie's] books is that it is possible to change other people's behavior by changing one's behavior toward them." Richard is living evidence of the accuracy of Carnegie's belief. He's fearless when it comes to initiating interactions with strangers. Even on elevators. And because he's self-assured and isn't looking for approval or validation—and is blessed with a quick and disarming sense of humor—people respond in kind.

"In kind." *In kindness.* I define "kindness" as any overture made from a compassionate heart with the intent to connect and include. This is my working hypothesis: *Approaching others with kindness without a personal agenda or the need to sell something* (yourself, a product, an idea or belief) *elicits kindness.*

At base, that's what this book is about. Kindness eliciting kindness.

This is how it works.

I'm with Richard picking up a few groceries while we're traveling. He's behind me, pushing the cart while I scan the shelves for needed items. There's an unattended, partially filled cart blocking a narrow aisle between the nut shelf and a produce display on a free-standing island. I scoot through, but the cart Richard is pushing won't fit past the one that's been temporarily abandoned. Instead of pushing it out of his way to another location where the person who left it would have to search to find it, he waits patiently until the missing shopper (another male) shows up. Richard greets him with a smile and says, "Good thing you got here, I was about to give you a ticket." The "offending" shopper responds in kind with "Thanks for giving me a break," to which my husband replies, "Actually, I'm out of tickets."

For a brief moment, two strangers, recognizing only that they were members of the human species, chose to acknowledge one another in a gentle and affirming way and created a healing ripple that spread into the world and made it a better place.

At least that's my story.

And speaking of story . . .

CHASING OUR TALES

Beware of the stories you read or tell; subtly, at night, beneath the waters of consciousness, they are altering your world.
—Ben Okri

Now we get to some sticky stuff.

Bottom-line observation: *Being different in the world required changing my story about myself to one that was empowering rather than self-defeating*. This is no easy task, but I can tell you from personal experience that it's essential.

Imagine a dog chasing its tail. You may have seen it and found it amusing. Around and around in a tight circle the dog goes, getting nowhere. That's us. Except we're not chasing our tails, we're chasing our tales. Tales about our life and our world. Tales about other people who share that world.

The difference between us and the dog is that our tales do get us somewhere. They get us in trouble if we don't know the difference between what is real and what we think is real. Our tales feed on themselves, strengthening with every retelling and embellishment until we're trapped inside our own heads.

Sadly, many of us will never stop chasing our tales. It's just what we human animals do. Our task is to remember that we are more than our tales and to not identify with them as "me": to not tell ourselves, "This is who I am."

We *have* tales, but we are not our tales. It's when we identify with them that we begin chasing them. Or being chased by them.

It All Begins with Story

Consider: From the moment before we take our first breath, we begin collecting input from our eyes, ears, nose, tongue, and skin. But it doesn't stop there. We're also born with a brain, the processing machine whose job it is to cobble together input from those sense organs and make meaning out of it that serves to keep us alive and functioning. The survival instinct cues us to literally cry for help when we feel discomfort in the form of hunger or pain.

For some period of time instinct rules, but being equipped with a cognizing brain, it's not long before we begin associating our behavior with predictable results. The meaning-making function of the brain kicks in. Crying means removal of discomfort: being picked up and held, food, a changed diaper, a smile. Loving care. Safety.

What Does It Mean?

I imagine the human brain reacts to the various sense impressions we receive and observations we make about ourselves and our environment the way it reacts when we dump the pieces of a jigsaw puzzle onto a table. It alerts us to begin sorting through the pieces with a single mission: to create meaning out of chaos by putting the pieces together so they make a cohesive, recognizable picture. But unlike the pieces of a jigsaw puzzle, which can be put together in only one way and always results in a duplicate of the picture that appears on the cover of the box, our sense impressions and observations are unique and can be put together to create an infinite number of "meaningful" stories.

Living in our own unique meaning-bubble, it's a wonder we can communicate at all. But given that we have no choice but to try, being aware of how our brains are compelled to make meaning through story gives us a chance to make a conscious choice in how we interpret an event.

It's an early February afternoon, sunny but cold—a chilling cold, the kind we get on clear winter days in the Northwest. I'm on my way to meet a friend at a downtown coffee shop, and I find a vacant parking spot half a block away. As I slow, pull to the curb, and begin backing into the space, I notice a young man with cropped sandy hair walking along the sidewalk: beardless, shoeless and shirtless; bare chest; arms and back a gallery of tattoos.

He stops and watches as I make an initial unsuccessful attempt to park, then begins gesturing with his hand to guide me into the spot and keep me from hitting the bumper of the car parked behind me. I smile and raise my hand in a gesture of thanks as my mind begins doing what minds do: create a story from the impressions we receive. His appearance has already primed me to label him a "street person" (with all the baggage that term carries for me), so I'm not surprised when he approaches the passenger-side window. His action adds weight to my suspicion that his "good deed" is a ploy to solicit money.

I get out of the car, pull out my wallet, and extract coins for the parking meter, plus two one-dollar bills. But instead of making a pitch for money, the young man draws my attention to the two feet of space between my car and the line marking the front of the parking spot. He suggests I might want to pull up a bit further to be sure the driver of the car parked behind me can get out. I thank him for his suggestion and ask if I can buy him a cup of coffee, offering the two singles. He accepts the bills graciously, bows, and thanks me for my kindness before continuing on his way.

I have no way of knowing whether this young man's action was designed to solicit a handout or whether he simply saw and responded to an opportunity to help an elderly woman park her car (maybe thinking about his grandmother), but it doesn't matter. The point is that a connection was made and a kindness was offered and received, enriching both our lives and perhaps those of others as we went about our business of the day. Had I gone with my initial suspicion that he was panhandling, ignored him and sat in my car until he moved on, it would have changed the trajectory and outcome of our encounter and created ripples of a different kind.

But I chose to tell myself a kinder story.

I suggest there can be no peace within ourselves and in the world at large until we understand the crucial role of story and how it influences our behavior. Things happen. Events occur. All completely neutral until a cognizing brain assigns meaning to them through story.

Imagine what a different world we'd live in if each person on the planet were to realize, accept, *and take responsibility for* the fact that every thought and action is a creative act that produces the "reality" they inhabit.

It boggles the mind.

Who Are You?

> ***We are what we think. All that we are arises with our thoughts. With our thoughts we make the world.***
>
> —Buddha. *The Dhammapada*

Because we're human, we're born storytellers. It's part of the basic human survival equipment wired into our brain. And storytelling is fun. We get to use our imagination by putting together stuff we've learned and stuff we think we remember. We get to make up any story we want about who we are—and about who the other people we share the planet with are.

Storytelling is fun until we start believing our stories are fact instead of fiction. We get into trouble when we use our made-up stories to define who we are and set the expectations we have of this made-up person we think of as "me."

I've been referring to myself as a "shy introvert," and I have in mind a solid picture of what that "means"—of the characteristics and manner that define a "shy introvert." Then, through selective attention, I look for other events that support and "prove" the identity I've assigned to myself. There is even a term in cognitive psychology for how this works. It's called *confirmation bias.* It refers to the tendency to select and interpret new data and experiences in a way that confirms our existing belief system.

This is a bad news/good news situation. The bad news is that once we've created an identity, good or bad, we set out to solidify this self-defined image of "who I am" and also of "who I am not." I'm not the person who can talk to strangers. I'm not the person who can act when I'm scared.

The good news is that stories can be changed. If we find ourselves living a life based on a negative story that creates separation, unhappiness, and loneliness, we can choose to acknowledge that our disempowering self-image is a product of our brain's programming—a computer error. We can reprogram ourselves by choosing to tell ourselves a different story about who we are and animating that new story by making different choices from the ones that are creating unhappiness.

A personal example is meeting Fred when I was in the beginning stages of dismantling my perception of myself as the person who is too shy to interact with strangers. When I first saw him, he was simply an old man, bent over the cane that was supporting him, walking slowly along the trail in front of me. As I passed him, I offered a simple "Good morning" and kept up my rapid pace to the break in the trail leading into the village. But as I left the shelter of the wooded trail and felt the cold wind whip about me, I changed my mind and decided to turn around and stay on the trail.

As I retraced my steps, I saw ahead of me the old man I'd passed earlier, who was now resting his arms on the wooden railing of a small bridge overlooking the creek that ran under the trail. I was conflicted. Aware of my self-generated story about being "the person deficient in social skills who has trouble talking to strangers" and, at the same time, wanting to acknowledge him, I said as I passed, "Nice day for a walk." He made a comment in response that I didn't catch.

Choice point: Do I let my default story prevail and keep walking? Or take a chance and stop?

I chose to stop. We talked for fifteen or twenty minutes, Fred and I. Contrary to the tale I'd been fabricating about him based on an initial assessment of his age and physical condition, he revealed himself as a bright, sparkly, educated, well-traveled man with delightful stories to tell about his ninety years on the planet.

I not only had an engaging and stimulating conversation on that walk, I challenged the disempowering story that I was a shy introvert unable or unwilling to interact with strangers. I'm not implying that it's easy to change stories we've lived with and reinforced over a lifetime, but every time we lean into our discomfort and make the harder choice, we weaken the old stories and free ourselves further from our allegiance to them.

Throw Out Your Label Maker

One way to avoid falling into the self-defining trap is to stop applying labels to ourselves based on selected data. When Walt Whitman said in *Song of Myself*, "Do I contradict myself? I am large. I contain multitudes," he was describing the human condition. Any label we pin on ourselves that casts us as being "that way" (good or bad in any of their incarnations) relegates us to the status of hero or villain in a soap opera or a comic strip. When we get stuck on a restrictive mental model of who we think we are, we deny the truth that we are, in fact, complex creatures: indeed, we are multitudes.

A former neighbor thinks I'm a kind person. She's both right and wrong.

One morning she called and asked if I'd drive her to the local walk-in clinic. She was experiencing symptoms in her chest that had her worried. She has a heart condition and didn't know whether it was her heart or just a panic attack. I, of course, took her, as I'm sure most people would if a neighbor asked for help. The willingness to help others in stressful conditions is part of our nature. (It was a panic attack; her heart was fine.)

I performed a couple of other "kindnesses" for her over the half-dozen years we were neighbors, which is the basis for her assessment of me. She didn't experience me when I did or said unkind things. Not that I'm intentionally unkind, but, as I assume happens for most of us, it happens occasionally when I'm not present and sensitive to the space or situation I find myself in.

The truth is that we tend to label people, especially those we have limited contact with, as the characteristic they manifest most often in our experience of them. We file them away in our mental filing cabinet under HONEST, KIND, CONSIDERATE, THOUGHTFUL, FAIR, COURAGEOUS, EMPATHIC—or ANGRY, UNJUST, UNFEELING, CRUEL. These are human characteristics we all display—or at least feel—on occasion. We do ourselves and others an injustice when we generalize the behaviors we observe and then label the one who manifests them as being *that way*: He's an angry person. She's a thoughtful woman. That child is a bully.

Yes, I sometimes act kindly, but that doesn't make me a kind person any more than making an unkind comment would make me an unkind person. We're wise to see both ourselves and others as the complex beings we are rather than as caricatures who animate only the behaviors we observe or focus our attention on.

Here's an example of how it works in real life.

At the top of my long to-do list is a trip to get groceries. Gray clouds hang over the city as I negotiate my way through the construction around the entrance to our apartment complex, delaying and complicating forays into the outside world.

By the time I make it to the interstate a half-mile away, my mood is as gray as the day.

It doesn't improve as I encounter heavy freeway traffic. I grit my teeth as a line of cars before me takes the same exit I'm taking, slowing me down further. Nor does circling the crowded store parking lot waiting for someone to vacate a space lighten my inner sky.

Inside the store, I maneuver aisles clogged with shopping carts pushed by other shoppers also focused on getting in and out as quickly as possible, their eyes scanning shelves for the next item on their list.

It isn't until I find myself standing in the bagged-nut aisle next to a slight, fragile-looking woman with short cropped gray hair who reminds me of my mother before she died at the age of ninety-eight that I allow my humanity to reassert itself. A head shorter than me, as my mother was, she's having difficulty seeing and reaching items on the top shelf. As it happens, we're looking for the same thing. As I take a bag of almonds to put into my cart, I ask her if it's what she's looking for. She graces me with a radiant smile as she acknowledges it is, remarking on how her short height prevented her from seeing them. I hand her the bag I'm holding, and she thanks me with another smile as we each continue with our shopping.

If someone had stopped this woman and asked about the person who had helped her find what she was looking for, she probably would have described me as "kind"—hardly a word appropriate to the thoughts and mood I'd manifested prior to our encounter, which would, if observed, have relegated me to a different drawer in her mental filing cabinet.

What You See Is What You Get

While a few of the checkers at my local supermarket have worked there as long as I've been a customer, there is also a fairly large turnover, which provides a lot of opportunity to practice with new employees some of the meet-and-greet behaviors I've been describing. But while I've become comfortable initiating interactions with checkers, my experience with other customers focused on loading their carts has been generally negative: heads down, attention on getting the job done and getting out. This discrepancy between the behavior of checkers and customers puzzled me until I realized that I was the constant in the equation. Like most of the customers, I was hurrying through the aisles intent on finding what I wanted and heading for the checkout stand. My eyes were either on the items on the shelves or on avoiding collisions with shopping carts that were in my way, ignoring those pushing them.

When I realized the role I was playing in the drama I'd been creating in which I was the star, I decided to do an experiment. On my next major shopping expedition, I relaxed my pace and intentionally looked at each shopper I encountered in the aisles, ready to smile and say good morning whenever there was eye contact. And there was a lot. By the time I checked out, I had given and received smiles and greetings at least a dozen times. Sometimes I initiated the exchange and sometimes another shopper made the first move.

Each time it happened I felt brighter and lighter. I had challenged my own story about why people were so closed and unfriendly by owning my own complicity and deciding to do something different.

I can't emphasize enough how empowering such a minor change in behavior can be. When I challenged my story about other shoppers being withdrawn and unfriendly by testing it literally in the marketplace, what I got was affirmation that other people are ready and waiting for a chance to connect. I also ratcheted up my confidence level, which made it easier to practice this new attitude and behavior the next time I went shopping, as well as on other occasions that took me beyond the safe walls of home.

Honoring Nature's Gift

Introverts are word economists in a society suffering from verbal diarrhea.
—Michaela Chung

The intent isn't to deny or try to change our introvert nature, but to recognize it has value and something to offer. Because introverts tend to be comfortable with silence and contemplation, when we do override our reticence and connect with others, we're less likely than our extrovert counterparts to overwhelm them with garrulous enthusiasm. We're more willing to give those we're interacting with psychological space.

At the same time, it's wise to acknowledge the potential downside of introversion: extreme self-consciousness. When I go into the world and find myself outside of my solitary "safe space," my tendency is to be so focused on myself and what others are thinking about me (a state of preening self-importance!) that I'm not present to anything but my own fear. I've reverted to my old "It's about me" story and let *me* eclipse *we*.

Our task is to honor and be grateful for the gifts of introversion while finding ways to share our inner richness with others through small acts of connection. Every time we step into our discomfort instead of avoiding it, we grow our confidence, and the world we inhabit benefits.

An example is a recent trip I made to the senior medical clinic. The receptionist met me with a smile as I took the chair before her at the counter. While she was checking me in, I was noticing that her lipstick and her silk blouse were the same shade of dark burgundy. When she looked up at me, I smiled and said, "Your lipstick and blouse match perfectly." She looked down at her blouse and laughed. "I always wear this lipstick," she said, "but I didn't notice that today I picked the same color blouse."

I left her still smiling and primed for the second act as I took a seat in the waiting room, noting a gentleman of my generation who was walking with the help of a cane from the entrance to the check-in counter. As he approached the receptionist, he said, with a twinkle in his voice and I imagine in his eye, "I'm here for a goodness check. I'm here to see how good I am."

It was a gloriously sunny spring day, and he'd brought the sunshine in with him.

That man chose to embrace his superpower: an upbeat spirit and a willingness to share it. We can do that. All it takes is being present to opportunities and a bit of courage, which grows every time we choose to shed our invisibility cloak and come out of hiding.

We never outgrow our basic disposition. I'm not going to change the fact that my genetic inheritance and early nurturance is that of an introvert who prefers and is fed by a quiet, contemplative existence. My small choices to connect and engage with people and offer kindnesses, as rewarding as they are, will always require me to push against my comfort envelope. And it's OK.

My life is ordinary, as yours may be. What's extraordinary is choosing to do the difficult thing and not let our fears and stories stop us from behaving in ways that serve something greater than our small, isolated selves.

This late-life new adventure I'm choosing is one where I *have* stories but I'm not *had by* them; where I can stand aside and observe them with lightness and humor, knowing they're a self-invented construct that I have the power to change at any time.

Keeping It Light

A sense of humor is a gift from the gods. It's probably the single most valuable attribute we possess for neutralizing our fear of engaging one another. If we were willing and able to see the absurdity of the situation we all find ourselves in as cognizant animals on a rotating rock floating in an incomprehensible vastness of space, we'd do the only reasonable thing: look at each other, laugh, and hug. Strangers no more in a very strange land.

Here's a story that illustrates one of life's absurdities that led to instant engagement with strangers.

I'm used to seeing people on the trail walking dogs, as dog walking seems to be a common motivation for dog owners to get some exercise. But if you were to guess what other animals I've encountered being walked, I suspect goats wouldn't be high on your list. Yet, one day, there they were coming toward me: two humans accompanied by a pair of goats.

As I approached the foursome, I noticed a man on a bicycle coming along the trail behind them. Nearing the group, he rang his bicycle bell to warn them of his presence.

The two goats promptly fell to the ground in a faint.

I stopped. The goat walkers stopped. The cyclist continued on his way. The goats got to their feet and shook themselves.

It was an instant conversation starter. Before we continued on our respective walks, the goat owners told me they're called "fainting goats" because when they're startled by unexpected movements or noises they fall to the ground in a faint, as I'd just witnessed. Fascinated, when I got home I checked Wikipedia for more information and found they're a goat species that "temporarily seizes when it feels panic. If startled by sudden movements or loud noises, they will attempt to escape from the disturbance . . . [causing] the goat to remain 'frozen' in the position that it was in previous to the attack, or . . . fall to the ground on its side."

To my knowledge, I've never fainted when confronted with social panic, but I sure know what it's like to freeze.

Checking In While Checking Out

Without awareness, it's impossible to escape my self-focused habit life and do something different. Unless I go into the world with the intention to connect and engage, and keep my attention alert for opportunities to act out that intention, I know it won't happen. I know this because I've observed in retrospect the many times I've stayed silent rather than engage.

Because I spend so much time in checkout lines, they're one of the best places for me to practice connection. To assist me in remembering my intention, I've trained myself to think of them as check *in* lines. As I approach the counter or begin unloading my purchases onto the conveyor belt, I check in with myself to see if I'm present in mind and body—conscious of where I am and who I'm with rather than off in storyland creating safe and soothing mind entertainment.

Pushing the Comfort Envelope

"Change your story, change your life" has become a popular notion—true, but incomplete. Here's a secret. It works both ways. You don't have to change your story to change your life. You can make a conscious choice to change your life first, and your action will begin changing your story about yourself, as happened for me when I met and conversed with Fred, the elderly gentleman on the trail. When I made the hard choice to step outside of my story and pushed against my comfort envelope, it both expanded my life options and added the word *courageous* to my self-definition.

For most of my life I've lived with the story that I'm just an ordinary person, and ordinary people don't do amazing or heroic things. Choosing to write a book at the age of eighty with no prior credentials required me to change my story to reflect that choice. My new story is that ordinary people *can* do extraordinary things. It doesn't require being somebody recognized as special, heroic, and larger than life.

Coming Apart at the Seems

Your assumptions are your windows on the world. Scrub them off every once in a while, or the light won't come in.
—Alan Alda

As we all know but tend to forget, things aren't always what they seem to be inside our heads. Pushing out of our comfort zone in order to interact with the world outside our mental stories requires breaking some of those "seems." One way to do that is to question assumptions.

When I was growing up in the first half of the twentieth century, before the advent of television, much less today's technological gadgetry constantly vying for our time and attention, mothers cooked from scratch and families sat down together for meals, a radical notion it seems today. Since I enjoy both cooking and eating, and trained as I was, I've happily taken on the responsibility of "home cooking" lunch and dinner for Richard and myself, but breakfast has evolved into a sort of do-it-yourself affair, allowing for different morning get-up times and routines. The "sort of" refers to my habit of making granola and a variety of scones and muffins to keep in the freezer for Richard to choose from when he's ready to take a break from his morning crossword and Sudoku puzzles.

One morning he chooses oatmeal-raisin scones. As I'm preparing my own breakfast, I notice a small pile of raisins on his plate next to the scones.

> Me: "Are there too many raisins in the scones? I'll put in fewer the next time I make them."
>
> He: "No. These are extras I got from the cupboard. I'm using them to sweeten the scones a little more instead of using jam." (He'd recently decided to cut down on the amount of sugar he eats.)
>
> Me: "Oh, I thought I'd put in too many."
>
> He: "I know that's what you assumed. Just keeping you on your toes."

I had made an accurate observation of the actual fact: My husband had a small pile of raisins on his plate. But my mental machinery didn't stop there. Without missing a beat, it jumped to assign meaning to what I had observed, resulting in a wrong assumption.

Had we not had the conversation, next time I made oatmeal-raisin scones I would have acted on my assumption and put in even fewer raisins.

Suppose we agree to question everything we think is real, everything we assume is true, everything we accept as solid, everything we dismiss the need to question, and accept all of it as just the way it is in the moment it occurs. Suppose we question every assumption we make before taking action based on it.

What effect would that have on our stories: about ourselves and about others?

The Fear Factor

You can only be afraid of
what you think you know.
—J. Krishnamurti

From my own experience, I can confidently state that my avoidance of interacting with other people, especially with strangers, is based on a self-generated fear-based story that warns me if I invite interaction I'll reveal something about myself that will be judged and found wanting. To paraphrase Krishnamurti, I'm afraid of what I think I know. The truth, of course, is that much of what I think I know, especially when my emotions are involved, is a fear-based construction.

For me, fear is the great energy depleter. If I find myself living a life where fear controls my behavior, my living essence is being held hostage by mind bandits. I'm caught in a fabricated story about who I am based on my past experiences and memories instead of being present to respond to what is happening in the *now* moment. When my experience of life tells me that I'm not capable of dealing with an unexpected and unpredictable event or situation without betraying my inadequacy, I panic. Withdrawal follows.

The Inner Bamboozle

Here's a final consideration in regard to story, beginning with a quote from Carl Sagan:

> *One of the saddest lessons of history is this: If we've been bamboozled long enough, we tend to reject any evidence of the bamboozle. We're no longer interested in finding out the truth. The bamboozle has captured us. It's simply too painful to acknowledge, even to*

ourselves, that we've been taken. Once you give a charlatan power over you, you almost never get it back.

Here's an even sadder thought: The greatest "bamboozling" takes place between our own ears. We have within us our own charlatan—our fearful "What about me?" storyteller extraordinaire ready to spin whatever tales are necessary to justify a choice to avoid relationship.

Here's how it works for me.

Well into the writing of this book, when I had a working draft, I registered for a workshop on publishing options. On the day of the workshop, I allowed for what I thought was ample time to find the venue on a local college campus, but got lost and was five minutes late. The instructor had begun introducing herself and interacting with the dozen people sitting in twos or threes at six oblong tables arranged three on a side with an aisle down the middle. Rather than draw attention to myself by taking a seat at a table toward the front, I sat at one of the empty tables in the back. Within the next five minutes, two other participants arrived and took seats in the front at the tables that already had occupants.

My fear-based choice set me up for being perceived by the instructor, the other members of the class—and myself—as an outsider. Me and them. When breaks occurred, tablemates chatted with each other, and during the lunch break wandered off in twos and threes. In typical introvert fashion, I asked no questions, made no contributions to the class conversation, and left having confirmed my story about being the loner: the outsider who doesn't belong and isn't "one of us."

Thus, from personal experience, I can recast Sagan's quote to read:

One of the saddest lessons of [our personal] *history is this: If we've bamboozled* [ourselves] *long enough, we tend to reject any evidence of the bamboozle. We're no longer interested in finding out what's true. The* [story-]*bamboozle has captured us. It's simply too painful to acknowledge, even to ourselves, that we've been taken* [by our own fear]. *Once you give* [your inner charlatan] *power over you, you almost never get it back.*

In spite of occasional "failures" to live up to my own higher possibility, I choose not to believe that the power of my own inner charlatan has captured me irrevocably. I take it as a warning and a challenge, not as an inevitability.

Seeing Clearly

Until my mid-forties, I had sharp vision, both near and far. I didn't appreciate it until it began to betray me as I neared the half-century mark. I reluctantly bought a pair of reading glasses at the local pharmacy, which worked for a while. At forty-nine I finally gave in and got my first pair of prescription glasses.

Once I got them, I began wearing them all the time, which turns out to have been a mistake because I now find myself viewing the world from the time I get up in the morning until I go to bed at night through miniature glass windows that perch on my nose and separate me from the real world—like I need another barrier.

But that's not all the bad news.

The only thing worse than wearing glasses all the time is wearing dirty glasses. And they get dirty all the time—from the inside as well as from the outside, usually right in the center, so everything I look at is slightly smudged. If you don't wear glasses, imagine sitting inside a rustic mountain lodge on an emerald green glacial lake nestled in the arms of towering snow-capped mountains. Now imagine floor to ceiling windows that every child guest has autographed with dirty fingers right at the vision line, separating you from a sharp perception of the natural glory of your environment.

But there's an upside.

Here's the good part about having dirty glasses—or a dirty window. It can serve as a reminder that, whether we wear glasses or not, we see the world through smudged, mentally fingerprinted minds. What we see through our mind's eye is often obscured and distorted by faulty ideas and opinions about ourselves, others, and the world we live in: a world shaped by our cultural conditioning and by religious, social, and political programming.

I clean my eyeglasses when I'm not seeing the physical world clearly. When I find myself on the field of life, I clean my mind by questioning the assumptions I bring to my witnessing. My goal is to draw no conclusions about what I'm observing and to give others the benefit of a doubt when I sense that my fear-based programming, opinions, and judgments are keeping me from relationship with them.

Not easy, but it's a goal I find worth pursuing.

WHAT CAN ONE PERSON DO?

I am only one,
But still I am one.
I cannot do everything,
But still I can do something;
And because I cannot do everything,
I will not refuse to do the something that I can do.

—Edward Everett Hale

Lighting a Candle in a Dark World

If we have a radio or television, read a newspaper, or surf news on a computer, tablet, or smartphone, we can't escape being assaulted—maybe to the point of paralysis—with horror stories: tragedy in the form of natural disasters that kill thousands; power politics run amok; families struggling to put food on the table and pay their mortgages and medical bills; gun violence on the streets, in theaters, churches and schools; a growing global pandemic. Sometimes it's tempting to pull down the shades and not get out of bed in the morning rather than face another day of bad news. The question "What can one person do?" seems justified.

Here's one answer to that question.

Our older son, Rick, tells a story about something that happened at a corporate event early in his career as a motivational speaker and entertainer. It was an evening event held in a tent on the beach of a Florida resort hotel. Part of his performance included mounting and riding a twelve-foot unicycle. On this occasion he was sitting on top of the unicycle when a dune buggy rider ran over the cord providing electricity to the tent, plunging it into darkness pierced only by small points of light from tea candles on the tables around which his audience sat. Rick suddenly found himself astride the unicycle on a three-foot-high stage, his body fifteen feet in the air without the sightline he needed for balance and to distinguish the edges of the platform. As his mind raced for a way to cope with his predicament and avoid its potentially disastrous consequence, a single point of light began moving toward him. One man had picked up a candle from his table and was walking toward the platform. His action signaled other guests to pick up the candles from their tables and join him. Together, surrounding the stage with their candles, the group provided enough light for Rick to successfully dismount from the unicycle.

One man's small act initiated a response that prevented what might otherwise have been a grievous end to the event.

The key here is presence and action. That man *was present* enough in that space to observe what was happening and know immediately what was needed, and he did it. He didn't second-guess himself or hesitate. He took appropriate action. His action prompted others to join him, and together they literally switched on the light in a dark space that held potential tragedy.

The Importance of Presence

Stay present. Introverts' minds tend to leave the present moment and go wandering . . . To be more present, try to experience the moment through your senses. Delight in the smell, feel, look, and taste of what is happening right now. When your mind starts to wander, bring it back to the sensations of the moment.

—Jenn Granneman

It's a quiet spring morning. Richard is off playing pool at the senior center while I sit at the kitchen table looking out through open sliding glass doors at the newly blossoming plants on the deck, watching squirrels cavort on the spring green lawn, listening to chatter of birds as they go about their bird business. I feel my butt sitting solidly on the chair, my sock-clad feet resting on the tiled floor, my hands cradling a cup of hot, freshly brewed tea.

This is heaven, and if you're a fellow introvert, you know exactly what I'm feeling. I could spend the entire morning just sitting here, being. Being what? Just *being*. Do extroverts get to experience this bliss?

But errands and appointments in the outside world await attention. A whole world of people exists outside of my quiet sanctuary. A world I've spent a lifetime trying to avoid and hide from.

But here's a secret. We introverts have something important to contribute to that world. We can take our *beingness* into it. And here's an even bigger secret. We can share it. What I'm suggesting is that when we're fully present with other people, they sense the fullness of our presence and have the opportunity to, in turn, be present with themselves and with us.

At base, learning to be present is learning how to relax: to release the tension that fear creates in mind (in the form of defensive stories) and in body (tight and rigid; ready for fight or flight). In essence, it's about being in the physical space we're occupying with full attention instead of in our heads creating stories about who we are in relation to who the "other" is and strategizing how to stay safe.

We can't be in relationship if we're not present.

The story of the quick and appropriate action of the man in the tent that sparked others' actions is a dramatic illustration of how the lighting-a-single-candle metaphor works in practice in a setting that allowed everyone who participated to see and feel the collective result of their small individual contribution. Most of us have to act on faith that our own small action contributes to a profound collective result.

Yes, we live in a world and at a time when it often appears that the darkness is overwhelming, catastrophe looms, and we're powerless to prevent it. Despair is a common reaction to the feeling of helplessness that accompanies the thought, What can one person do? But like the man in the tent, we *can* do something. We can stay present in our lives, alert to opportunities to let a smile be the small candle of kindness we offer to others in whatever situation we find ourselves, trusting our action may in turn spark their own offerings to others.

Who knows? Our joint effort may switch on the light of love and compassion in a dark world and save us all. At the very least, we'll light up our own life and the lives of those we reach out to in a spirit of lovingkindness.

10 WAYS TO SMILE AT STRANGERS

We can bring positive energy into our daily lives by smiling more, talking to strangers in line, replacing handshakes with hugs, and calling our friends just to tell them we love them.

—Brandon Jenner

Here are ten ways to smile at strangers that extend beyond the physical act. Some are small gestures involving little risk and having only a temporary effect, although we can never tell what impact a simple gesture of connection and acknowledgment may have on the recipient—or on the world. Other efforts may require going outside—maybe far outside—our comfort zone, but have potentially huge payoffs.

We begin with the simple act itself.

1. **Just smile.**

We shall never know all the good that a simple smile can do.

—Mother Teresa

I tried many titles for this book before hitting on the one that brought bright smiles to the faces of the people on my informal editorial team. When I found the Steve Maraboli quote "Smile at strangers and you just might change a life," it verified my hunch that smiling at strangers is the key to instant connection. Having tested it out, I'm ready to suggest it may be the simplest action we can take in disarming the sense of separation and fear of "the other" that appears to be chronic in our Western culture, particularly in the United States at this point in our history. I truly believe that a genuine, heartfelt smile is one of the greatest gifts we can give to others with whom we share the planet.

In a blog post in *Psychology Today* titled "There's Magic in Your Smile," author Sarah Stevenson explains how it works for her. She's having a tough morning and stops at a neighborhood French café for a cup of tea on her way to a doctor's appointment.

She writes: "As I sit under my little gray cloud, my pretty, young server, Colette, flashes me a dazzling smile that sticks there for the entire interaction. I can't help but smile back . . . Suddenly, my day doesn't seem so bad. I finish my tea and head to my appointment equipped with a grin on my face, feeling as though I've slipped on a pair of rose-colored glasses. Today's lesson? It turns out that when I smile, the world smiles back."

In another *Psychology Today* article, I found reference to a study in which half of the individuals in a waiting room were allowed access to their smartphones while the second half were not. Not surprisingly, those holding their phones were less likely to smile at others. Based on my own experience, I'm willing to extend that finding and suggest they're also less likely to even notice those they share the space with.

2. **Unplug in public spaces.**

"Plugged in, tuned out." A familiar phrase and perhaps an experience that many of us are all too familiar with: being alone in a crowd trading personal connection with those we're sharing physical space with for the virtual world we're plugged into. Michael Meade, in his book *Awakening the Soul*, refers to "the rise of 'connective' technologies that contribute to deep disconnections while 'linking' people at surface levels of life."

One morning I need to have some blood drawn for some lab work. When I arrive at my local lab facility, I notice a woman standing to one side of the entrance, her back to me, talking on her phone. I enter the tiny, four-chair waiting room and find two more people—a man and a woman—sitting across from each other, heads down, each busy with their smartphones. Neither of them looks up or acknowledges my arrival.

The woman I saw outside comes in, takes the empty seat, and begins scrolling on her phone. Ignoring the stack of seriously outdated gossip magazines beside me, I choose to wait in silence.

Each of my three silent companions is called in turn for their blood draw, leaving me alone in the waiting room for less than a minute before a man of my generation enters: late seventies or early eighties, portly, in overalls, with hair as thin and gray as my own. He sits in the chair beside me. He doesn't pull out a cell phone.

"It's good to see someone who isn't plugged in," I say. "I've been sitting here with three people who never looked up from their phones while they were waiting."

"I bought a smartphone a couple months ago," my new companion replies. "Took it back after two weeks and got a flip phone. Decided I don't want one of those things."

We continue chatting until I'm called into the lab, which terminates our brief conversation. On my way out he's still waiting.

"Good talking to you," I say as I leave.

"You too," he says with a smile.

Connecting and engaging with strangers, however briefly, demonstrates that we're more than the machines we so readily pledge our allegiance to.

3. **Note nametags on service personnel and acknowledge them by name.**

What's in a name? Name researcher H. Edward Deluzain, in his article "Names and Personal Identity," concludes that "the sense of personal identity and uniqueness that a name gives us is at the heart of why names interest us and why they are important to us as individuals and to our society as a whole."[1]

When I began my project to offer kindnesses to people I encountered in public places, I began noting the nametags of salespeople and service personnel in stores, the post office, the library, the bank, and other places where I did business. Then I used the name of the person as I thanked them for their service. At first I found this hard to do. I felt self-conscious and awkward. It seemed too intimate. But I persisted, and was surprised at how quickly the awkwardness and discomfort were replaced by an easeful and

1 https://www.behindthename.com/articles/3

genuine act of acknowledgment. Now it feels uncomfortably incomplete to me to offer thanks to someone wearing a nametag without acknowledging them personally. Using their name communicates, I see you as a whole person who has a unique life beyond the function you're serving.

A name is a mark of identity. Some people like their names, some don't, but everyone has a personal relationship to their own name. When I see a name on a nametag that's unusual, I give it special attention, acknowledging that I see and register it. By extension, it communicates that I see and acknowledge the person the name belongs to. Sometimes I repeat it and add, "Nice. I like that." Again, by extension I'm saying, "I like you."

If it's not clear how to pronounce the name, I ask its owner how they pronounce it. The most unusual name I've encountered is Nevaeh. When I asked the hotel clerk wearing the nametag about it, she told me it's heaven spelled backwards, her original birth name given to her by her mother. It was clear that she loved her name and was happy to have someone ask about it so she could tell them its origin.

Look at the nametag of the grocery checker, the bank clerk, the postal worker, the nurse's assistant, or the front desk attendant as you encounter them doing their jobs. Instead of a generic "Thanks," make it personal. "Thanks, Tori," "Thank you, David," "Thanks so much, Charlene." Notice the difference in how *you* feel when someone addresses you by name: how much more you feel connected, even if the person is a stranger, especially if the use of your name is accompanied by eye contact, a smile, and genuine warmth.

One incident in particular sold me on how important it is to acknowledge by name people who serve us. It happened on a supermarket trip when I arrived at the checkout stand with a full shopping cart. The young female checker greeted me and asked if I had any special plans for the day. I hesitated, laughed, and told her apparently not special enough to have them jump immediately to mind.

As the two of us exchanged simple pleasantries, a young man who looked to be in his late teens was quietly bagging my groceries. I noted his nametag as the checker was handing me my receipt, and when he had finished loading my cart I smiled and gave him a breezy "Thanks, Cameron" as I began pushing the cart toward the exit doors. Behind me I heard a surprised, "Oh, you know my name." Half turning, I smiled and lifted my arm in acknowledgment as I walked away. It didn't surprise me when, on a subsequent shopping trip, I noticed Cameron, who was bagging that day, move to the stand where I was checking out.

There's a woman who weighs and accepts payment for produce at one of my regular stops at the farmers market. Because she doesn't wear a name tag, I got in the habit of offering only a smile and thank you when paying for my purchases. While she wasn't impolite, she wore a rather stern expression and seldom offered more than quick answers to direct questions. One day I heard someone call her by name as I was approaching the stand. I gathered my purchases and took them to the counter as always, but this time, as I handed her the produce I greeted her using her name and made a comment about how much I appreciated being able to buy fresh produce. She looked at me (the first time she'd made direct eye contact), offered a shy smile with my change, and told me she didn't understand why anyone would buy packaged produce in the summer with so much available fresh from the fields. We're not exactly old friends now, but she graces me with a smile each time I stop by her produce stand.

4. **Ask provocative questions of people you typically interact with only superficially.**

   I discovered this one accidentally when, on a quiet afternoon when I was the only customer in the checkout line of a local market, I asked the checker what she does when she isn't working. Her eyes lit up, and with a full-on smile she said, "Sew!" She went on to tell me about the sideline sewing business she was building. Since that first brief interaction, every time I go through her checkout line I ask how her new business is going. It always elicits a mood change that enlivens her expression and body posture, and she always thanks me for asking.

   As it turns out, the What do you do when you're not working? question works well in grocery store checkout lines when I've got a full cart and find myself waiting while the checker is scanning my purchases. Usually I get generic responses, like: Watch TV. Play video games. Go out with my friends. Spend time with my kids [or grandkids]. But the question is worth asking for the few times when spines straighten, faces take on a glow, and eyes begin to sparkle, as happened with the checker who said without hesitation, "Sew!"

   Other successes include a middle-aged male checker whose checkout line I'd been through often but had never engaged beyond the usual niceties. The day I asked him what he did in his off time, his quiet demeanor came alive as he told me that when he wasn't working he was taking his daughter, a passionate, award-winning gymnast (she began at the age of two) to gymnastic meets and competitions. He continues to keep me updated on her budding gymnastic career whenever I go through his checkout line and ask about her.

Another payoff came when I asked the question of a part-time checker who was unfailingly pleasant and interactive whenever I went through his line. He told me he painted and had an exhibition coming up at a Seattle gallery. He'd been working shifts at the market for several years to pay the bills until he could support himself with his painting. As I was leaving, he thanked me for asking. I haven't seen him checking groceries since. I'm hoping the Seattle exhibition was a success and that he's now doing what he loves full time.

In my experience, most people are starved for acknowledgment of who they really are and of what truly matters to them. They want to be seen and heard. (Don't we all?) Give them that opportunity.

5. **Be generous with compliments.**

Although we often assume otherwise, people don't know what we're thinking. When you notice something you like or appreciate about someone, open your mouth and tell them.

"I wish all parents treated their children the way you do yours. You have such respect for them."

"I appreciate what you said in the meeting this morning. It showed me a new way to look at the problem we've been having."

"What a pretty color your blouse is. That shade of blue makes your eyes sparkle."

The first task in finding opportunities to give compliments is being alert. As I've already suggested, this means being present in time and place. What are you paying attention to when you're standing in line at the post office, the DMV licensing counter, the customer service counter? If you're like me, you're in your head a galaxy away from where your physical body is located. (It's not called being "spaced out" for nothing.) You're trying to escape the mundane world. And it *is* mundane until we open ourselves to the magic of the present moment. Then we're available to notice we're not alone. We notice the T-shirt with the clever message, the classy car that's just pulled in beside us in the mall parking lot, the baby in the stroller smiling up at us. We notice and allow ourselves to respond. We make an appreciative comment as the teen driver gets out of his car. We smile and wiggle our fingers at the baby, who giggles in response, triggering a return smile from the mother for the stranger noticing her child and may even lead to a brief verbal interchange as we await our turn at the pharmacy counter. We compliment the clerk with the exotic hairdo or the elegant handwriting. These are all forms of communicating, I see you. I acknowledge you. I appreciate you as a unique person.

Opportunities for offering compliments abound once we become alert for them.

Well into the writing of this book, when I was feeling good about my growing ability to interact with strangers in public places, I found myself standing in a supermarket line behind a young girl—slight in stature, likely in her teens—holding a gift card and two small items. Her facial expression and body posture suggested shyness as she quietly waited for the customer ahead of her to complete his transaction. Although I wasn't in a hurry, I wasn't feeling relational, and I made no attempt to engage either her or the woman behind me unloading her cart.

What I *was* feeling was the discomfort of missing an opportunity to walk my talk.

Choice point: Do I let myself off the hook and accept that this is one of those times that my default behavior wins out? Or challenge myself to make the extra effort of breaking the mood of isolation I was sensing both in myself and in those around me?

As I was considering my situation, I was watching the teenager facing the counter in front of me, patiently and quietly awaiting her turn. I noticed she was wearing jeans and a black scoop neck T-shirt imprinted with owl faces. Around her neck was a turquoise crystal pendant on a gold chain. She hadn't looked at me since I'd joined the line, and although I'm usually reluctant to address someone with whom I haven't had eye contact, I found myself saying, "Your pendant is lovely." She turned and looked and me, and the impression I got was of a mannequin coming to life. She graced me with a bright smile and alert eyes as she thanked me. I asked if she'd made the pendant herself, and she told me she hadn't but had found it in a jewelry boutique and fell in love with it. After she'd completed her transaction at the counter, she smiled at me as she left. I passed on her smile to the checker as I interacted with her in a brighter mood than the one I'd entered the line with.

Being willing to speak up and compliment others is easier when we remember how good it feels to receive an unexpected compliment ourselves, as happened to me on a senior discount day at a local market. It had snowed the night before—atypical for the coastal Northwest—and people were beginning to dig out. I usually try to get to the store early on discount day to avoid the midday crowds that typically fill the aisles, but because of the weather, the store was only lightly populated when I got there near noon. Shopping cart leading the way, I headed to the fresh seafood counter and requested a salmon filet.

As I was turning away from the counter, filet in hand, I found myself looking into a pair of blue eyes crinkled not by age but by youthful playfulness. They belonged to a young man I guessed to be in his early twenties, wearing baggy jeans and a gray short sleeve T-shirt—a generic looking young man I wouldn't normally have noticed in a group and most certainly wouldn't have expected to notice me.

But this bright-eyed young man was not only looking at me, he was smiling. Nodding toward my teal coat, he said, "That's a great color on you," then added, "and your eyes are beautiful."

Startled and caught completely off guard, I found myself spontaneously matching his broad smile and saying, "Thank you. You're a sweetheart," as I put an acknowledging hand on his shoulder and stepped away, making room for him to move forward. A *pas de deux* at the seafood counter.

Had I been in a suspicious frame of mind and caught in the story I often tell myself about being old and invisible, undeserving of attention, I might have discounted the young man as an employee of the store assigned to randomly compliment elderly customers on senior discount day. Making a choice to accept his gesture as genuine allowed a connection to be made that brightened not only my day, but undoubtedly his, and perhaps that of those who witnessed our exchange.

It warms my heart to know there are people like this young man in the world spreading joy.

6. **Be kind to a pet or a child.**

One of the best and surest ways to make contact with a stranger is to notice and be kind to their dog or child. The caveat is that while you can sometimes get away with playing social games with an adult, it doesn't work with children. Just as animals can sense fear, children know when they are being patronized and, if they haven't been shamed into silencing their innate wisdom, have no qualms about letting us know they don't appreciate it.

Case in point: I was out for a walk on a wet and blustery late fall day, the sidewalk littered with decaying leaves, the chill air scented by wood smoke from fireplaces pressed into early use. Approaching me was a mother holding the hand of a young child, a boy who looked to be three or four. He was wearing a bulky gray nylon jacket and a gray knit hat with two huge ears. He resembled a cartoon mouse.

As we met, I paused, smiled, and said to the boy, "What cute ears you have." He stopped, looked up at me, pulled off the hat, pointed to his ears, and said in a tone suggesting a teacher addressing a slow student, "These are my ears. This is a hat," shaking it at me to be sure I understood the difference.

In his wise innocence, this child knew and was willing to speak the truth. He wasn't intimidated by an adult who was either a bit demented or, worse, being condescending by treating him as if he were incapable of distinguishing between a hat and human ears. He stepped up to what was required of him in the moment by articulating clearly and simply the distinction I had apparently missed. In short, he was inviting me into relationship with him as an intelligent and unique individual. If I had recognized him as such, I would more appropriately have said something such as "I like your hat. It looks like you have mouse ears. It must be fun to wear."

A few months later, the universe gave me an opportunity to put that thought to the test. I was on the trail heading home from a walk when I noticed a man, a woman, and a small child a short distance ahead of me. The woman was holding the boy's hand, and on his head was a brown knit hat sporting a pair of dog ears that bounced as he walked. When I spotted the young family, I was nearing a junction where I normally take a side trail into my apartment complex. But on this day I chose to stay on the main trail.

As I moved toward the family, the man and woman paused by a railing to look down at the creek that bordered the trail. The young boy, dog ears flopping, was running back and forth behind them as I approached. Smiling, I pointed to his hat and said, "I like your hat. I bet it's fun to wear." The child, shyer than the mouse-hat boy (demonstrating introvert/extrovert personalities even at a young age) ran to his mother's side and hid his face in her coat. His father picked up the conversational ball and tossed it back to me. "And it's fuzzy and warm inside. I'd like to wear it myself," he playfully offered. “Me too,” I replied. “At my age, I think I could get away with it.”

Both parents laughed and wished me a good day. The universe was smiling.

On another occasion, I was cutting through a parking lot coming home from the village when a small white terrier, walking its owner, stopped and began tugging on its leash in my direction. I’ve never had a dog and am generally uncomfortable around them. My story is that they’re unpredictable, and my reaction when a dog is near is to keep a safe distance between me and the animal.

But this time I made a different choice and walked toward the terrier. Seeing me approach, the man said to the dog, “Do you want to visit?”

I stooped, patted the wriggling body, and cupped the dog’s face in my hands. “He or she?” I asked.

“He,” the portly gentleman attached to the other end of the leash replied, with a friendly smile.

“What’s his name?”

“Bubba.”

“Hi Bubba,” I said to the dog, looking into his eyes as I continued petting him. “Who’s walking who?” I asked his human companion.

“He always wins” was the reply.

Two humans and a dog, connecting. One woman, changing her story about herself.

7. Reach out and touch someone.

To touch is to give life.
—Michelangelo

At a recent social event that Richard and I attended, another guest—a man neither of us knew—appeared to be looking for a fight. His language, tone, and body language were aggressive and in-your-face as he confronted a woman who had expressed a political opinion contrary to his own. As we watched him become more agitated in response to the woman's calm refusal to engage, Richard leaned toward me and said, "He needs a hug."

Probably not the first response most of us would suggest while witnessing such a scene, but perhaps the most discerning. What's your first impulse when your child or grandchild is upset and out of control? You give them a reassuring hug. This man was animating his scared inner child.

The incident got me thinking about whether the lack of warm, affirming physical contact sometimes expresses itself as aggressive behaviors such as this man was enacting. *Please see me. Please touch me. Please love me.*

I wonder about the lack of opportunities to touch and be touched in a culture where so many people, especially the elderly and housebound, are unpaired and living alone. Research has revealed the severe negative effects on babies and children in institutional settings who are left untouched except for routine, scheduled feedings and clothing changes. Why should it be different for those at the opposite end of life?

In his article "Hands on Research: The Science of Touch," published in 2010 in the online *Greater Good Magazine,* researcher Dacher Keltner tells us, "A pat on the back, a caress of the arm—these are everyday, incidental gestures that we usually take for granted . . . But after years spent immersed in the science of touch, I can tell you that they are far more profound than we usually realize: They are our primary language of compassion, and a primary means for spreading compassion. In recent years, a wave of studies . . . is suggesting that touch is truly fundamental to human communication, bonding, and health."

A touch can be anything from a light hand on the shoulder to a bear hug. Some people seem to be natural huggers, while others shy away from the intimacy of full body contact and limit themselves to half hugs or limp handshakes if physical contact is expected.

Yet touch is an area that requires discrimination. Knowing when a touch is needed and appropriate is a felt response rather than a mentally calculated one. It happens spontaneously in response to a present moment event or situation. The body knows and acts before the mind rides in leading its cavalry of "should" stories that leave us confused and hesitant. These are the times when we're most likely to act inappropriately.

It would most likely be inappropriate for the woman being confronted by the angry guest at the social event to step forward and give the man a hug, even if she were inclined to. But perhaps it would be both appropriate and welcomed if in passing by him later in the evening she was, in that moment, moved to lightly touch him on the shoulder.

A final note: If you're fortunate enough to have a partner, friends, or family members you're comfortable enough with to exchange hugs, count your blessings and take advantage of opportunities to give and receive them.

8. **Answer phone calls with a vocal smile.**

Think of what an immediate lift it is when you initiate a call and the person you reach answers in a bright, upbeat manner—and how dispiriting it is when the response is curt and cold. It may be impersonal, but it *feels* personal. OK, it might be a stretch to be upbeat and warm when the caller is a fundraiser or is making a sales pitch, but try to remember that they're doing a job that likely entails being frequently hung up on and perhaps verbally abused many times a day. I find it helps to think of how I would feel if someone I love—one of my children or grandchildren—had to make a living this way and was treated in the manner in which many of us respond to fundraisers and telephone salespeople. It's possible to say no without dehumanizing the caller. Richard is a great role model for how to do this. He always takes a minute or two to engage callers who want to sell him something (a product, a candidate, a belief) in a brief interchange that acknowledges the caller as a fellow human being trying to put bread on the table, even as he firmly but politely declines what they're offering.

Another way to deliver a smile in a more unique (and introvert friendly) manner is to respond to a text to which no response is required or expected.

A few weeks away from voting day in a local election I got a text that read: "Hi Nancy, this is Blaine volunteering w/ . . . Records show that you signed the petition to get . . . on the ballot . . . I'm texting to thank you and make sure you're ready to vote."

My first response was to ignore it and go about my other business. Then, on a sudden impulse, I texted back: "Thanks for doing this work, Blaine. You can count on my vote." Within seconds I received a reply. Actually, two of them. The first was: "Sweet!" The second, quick on its heels, was: "You're welcome," accompanied by a smiley face icon.

I allowed myself to imagine that my response was the only one this young man received, and that being acknowledged and thanked for his efforts fueled the volunteer job he'd taken on. A small pebble dropped in another's pond, creating ripples of connection and good will that extended who knows how far?

9. **Just listen.**

Introverts have a superpower: listening.
—Jenn Granneman

Being heard is so close to being loved that for the average person they are almost indistinguishable.
—David Augsburger

Doris Lessing, in *The Golden Notebook*, echoes Augsburger's wisdom: "Do you know what people really want? Everyone, I mean. Everybody in the world is thinking: I wish there was just one other person I could really talk to, who could really understand me, who'd be kind to me. That's what people really want, if they're telling the truth."

In interactions with others, one of the greatest kindnesses we can offer is to just listen without filtering what we're hearing through a story. Perhaps you know from personal experience the healing influence of feeling truly heard without fear of judgment—a time when you've opened your heart and talked out what's troubling you to a trusted friend or family member. That's the basis and practice of talk therapy.

I found myself in a position to offer such "therapy" on an occasion a couple of years ago in the shared laundry facility of our apartment complex. A man who appeared to be in his mid-forties was loading laundry into a washer when I arrived to retrieve my dried clothes. After a few moments of silence as we each attended to our laundry tasks, I offered some routine pleasantry such as "It always feels good to get the laundry done." In response, he told me he wasn't used to doing his own laundry. I asked him if he was a new resident.

That was all it took. He told me that his wife had recently asked for a divorce, and at her request he'd moved out of the family home he'd shared with her and their two teenage children. He was clearly troubled, his sadness reflected in his face and posture, tears just a blink away.

For the next half hour I just listened as he told me about his shock and the disorientation he felt in response to his wife's request. He'd suggested marital counseling, which she'd declined to consider. Most of all, he told me about the heartbreak of being separated from his children. Although he talked with them on the phone frequently and saw them on weekends, he was no longer a part of their daily lives.

As he talked, quiet tears came. I offered no advice or comments, just put my laundry aside, made eye contact, and listened. Before we parted, he thanked me and said I was a "good listener."

Over the next several months, we encountered each other occasionally in the laundry or mailroom or on the sidewalk between buildings coming or going. I always asked how he was, and he'd tell me about his children: when he'd seen them and how they were doing.

Then one day he was coming down the stairs from his apartment as I was passing by. When he saw me, his face lit up, and he stopped and shared his good news. He and his wife had been seeing a counselor, and she'd asked him to move back home. Soon after, I noticed there was a new tenant in his former apartment.

I hope he and his wife have become better listeners.

Listening connects us and heals the hurt we carry— we can make a world of difference for one another by listening.

—Patty Wipfler

10. **Share the good news.**

As I write this, I'm sitting at my kitchen table watching a young woman standing on the sidewalk across the courtyard as she looks up at a second-story apartment unit that's been recently vacated. She's holding a cell phone to her ear and suddenly begins stamping her feet, jumping up and down, and dancing in circles in the lightly drizzling rain. A pause—then more dancing and stamping. She hangs up and initiates another call, talks for a minute or two, takes photos of the exterior of the unit, and dances away toward the rental office.

It's not hard to put the pieces together and create a good news story. The first call was from the office, confirming she had the rental. Rentals are hard to come by in Bellingham, and our complex always has a waiting list. Hence, the dancing. The second was sharing the good news with someone important to her. Maybe a friend or partner who will share the apartment.

Watching this happy young woman, I smile and feel my mood lift. Her joy and excitement are infectious. Lucky are those she shares her good news with. They too stand to benefit.

Which reminds me of another good news story.

It began with a simple observation to a checker at the store where I do much of my food shopping. I mentioned the unusual lack of traffic in the store. The aisles were nearly empty, and there were only two checkout stands open, with one or two customers in each. Not a typical shopping experience at one of the most popular food stores in town. It was late autumn, and Robert, the checker, speculated that the late-season warm and sunny weather was keeping people outside rather than shopping.

As he scanned and bagged my groceries, he told me that personally he woke up every day hoping for rain. Not a usual wish for a Northwest resident. But Robert is a gardener, and his summer crop was suffering the extended drought July and August had brought that year. I asked him what he grew in his garden, and he listed the vegetables it was producing. My question and focused attention signaled my interest, and he proceeded to tell me about the produce exchange his wife had initiated with other neighbors who also have gardens. Once a week they all get together and exchange the literal fruits of their labors, sharing excesses with elderly neighbors who don't have access to fresh vegetables.

I left grateful for a good news story that brightened my day even beyond what the weather gods had provided.

As for the world at large . . .

It's all too easy to let pessimism and a What's the use? attitude become our default mode when the media are focused on scare stories. Although love may ultimately conquer all, fear wins out every time when it comes to attention-getting headlines and securing advertising dollars. A daily media diet devoid of the milk of human kindness and compassion is a sure way to invite malnutrition of the soul.

The good news is that healthy alternatives are available. It may be more work to find upbeat stories than to let our attention be captured by negative headlines on cable news stations or our daily newspaper, but those stories are out there shining light into the darkness of media fear-mongering. If you need help in finding them, plug "good news stories" into your browser. Find a site (or several) you like, and subscribe to offset the ubiquitous media assaults of bad news.

These are only a few of the ways you can bring the light of kindness into a dark world. The key to actions that brighten the life of another is to think about what lights up your own life. Under what circumstances are your spirits lifted? What acts performed by another pierce the darkness of your feeling of disconnection and aloneness, if only for a moment or two? Then do those things for others. Remember the man in the tent with the tea candle, and trust that every small act makes a difference.

If you're impatient and lighting tea candles isn't enough, here's a radical suggestion you might consider: Discover and own what lights your inner fire, what's juicy and alive in you and waiting to be turned loose. Then go for it. When we do that, we become not just a pinprick of light in the darkness, but a blazing bonfire.

Becoming a New Being: Patience Required

What you are, the world is. And without your transformation, there can be no transformation of the world.

—J. Krishnamurti

After I had completed a draft of this book that I felt was ready for test readers, whatever muse had been fueling my writing went on vacation. No new insights, no writing, and, of most concern, little impetus to engage others and create new stories of connection. I was failing to practice what I'd been preaching, which invited a heavy rain of self-judgment and doubt.

When I find myself falling into these pits of self-blame and despair, I remind myself that, unlike in fairy tales, transformation into a "new being" doesn't occur with the wave of a wand or a wizard's *abracadabra.* It requires disciplined practice over time. It's not dissimilar to building a strong and healthy body through a lifetime of educated and intelligent choices. It happens through a persistent and reliable commitment followed up with sustained practice and patience. Part of the process is allowing for what appear to be fallow periods. Those periods are essential for absorption and digestion to take place while growth is stabilizing.

We can rest assured that if we're making a sustained and committed effort to grow into a "new being," transformation will occur. When it does, the entire world benefits. As Krishnamurti reminds each of us, "What you are, the world is."

MAKING A DIFFERENT CHOICE

Stories of Connection

All you have to do is, for one instant, stop fighting to sustain your separation, and there is only what is. It is quite simple.
—Lee Lozowick

What keeps us from connecting with others through small acts of acknowledgment and kindness? The stories we tell ourselves: It won't make a difference. I don't know what to say. It makes me uncomfortable. I'm too busy. What if he/she doesn't respond?

Been there, done that. I know them all. And I know there's a more fulfilling way.

Flying High

My default mode when I travel is to limit my interaction with others to the polite pleasantries exchanged with airport personnel and fellow travelers and to otherwise fade into the background of the crowd. On a flight home from visiting friends and family in Arizona,

I made a conscious choice to be present and available for engagement with the people I encountered during my day of travel.

Phoenix's Sky Harbor International Airport presented plenty of opportunities to test my resolve. One of the first occurred when I noticed a fit-looking elderly man sitting on the floor with his back against a wall near the gate I was heading toward. He had a pile of what looked like climbing gear beside him and was quietly watching the foot traffic. Rather than pass him by, as other travelers were doing, I stopped and commented on his unorthodox choice of seating. We chatted briefly, and as I moved on he raised a hand in acknowledgment of my noticing him and taking the time to stop.

Buoyed by this small success, when I arrived at the gate and waited to board my flight, I kept my book in my backpack and stayed available for the kind of small talk engagement Richard is so good at. There were ample opportunities as boarding took place. Once I made the choice to be present and broke the ice for those in the boarding line, others joined in, and I found myself chatting with several of my fellow passengers.

But the best was yet to come. If you're an airline traveler, you know there is no greater test of your relationship skills than sitting shoulder to shoulder with a stranger (or two, if you're traveling alone and happen to be in a middle seat) on a multi-hour flight. I favor window seats both because I like to look at the landscape below and because being tucked into a corner affords the illusion of a bit more privacy.

On this particular flight, a plump grandmotherly type woman in an aisle seat had to rise to let me maneuver myself into the window seat. Her look and manner invited interaction, and we exchanged brief comments about choosing seats at the back of the plane to increase the possibility of having the middle seat unoccupied. (It was a Southwest flight and seats are not assigned.)

I took the novel I'd brought for the nonstop flight to Seattle out of my backpack and called Richard to make arrangements for him to pick me up. As we were talking, a middle-aged Hispanic man worked his way into the middle seat. When I closed my phone, instead of opening my book and settling into my corner, I spontaneously turned to him, put my hand on his shoulder, and said, "Welcome to the best seat on the plane." The woman in the aisle seat laughed, and our new seatmate beamed a radiant smile while communicating in broken English that he didn't speak the language. It didn't matter. My light and friendly comment had established an instant connection among the three of us. As we waited for the plane to take off, he took out his phone and showed us photos of his daughter, her husband, and the new grandchild he was going to see.

As the woman on his other side and I settled into our reading, our seatmate pulled out the airline magazine and began doing the Sudoku puzzles. I noticed over the course of the next hour that he was working them quickly. When he had finished them all, he put the magazine back and sat quietly as we were served snacks and drinks.

After the stewardess had collected our waste materials and before I resumed my reading, I took my iPad out of my backpack, hit the Sudoku icon, and offered it to the gentleman sitting quietly beside me. He graced me with his glowing smile as he gladly accepted the iPad. I watched as his hand hovered over the levels of play before choosing the medium option. After a few games, he changed the level to hard. He may not have been able to speak English (and isn't it all too easy to assume that if someone doesn't speak "our" language they're mentally impaired), but there was no doubt in my mind that this man had me hands down in brain power, at least when it comes to Sudoku puzzles.

But the story doesn't end there. At the end of the flight, as we were gathering our carry-on items and making our way into the aisle, he offered me his hand. I took it, and as we were shaking hands, he said, in heartfelt English, "God bless you."

I thanked him, and we made our way down the aisle. He was ahead of me, and when we got to the gate concourse he seemed unsure about where to go. I pointed the way toward the baggage claim area, and we walked together. When we arrived at the carousel, he was met by a man about his own age. As they greeted each other in Spanish, my flight companion gestured toward me. The second man shook my hand, smiling and nodding his thanks.

Another handshake and a second blessing, and we parted, having made a human connection that enriched not only us but perhaps created ripple effects that benefited those we encountered as we went our separate ways.

Coffee with a Smile

On the Southern California trip where I'd had the pleasant encounter with a groundskeeper at the rental complex where Richard and I were staying, I developed a morning writing routine that began with a twenty-minute walk to a 7-Eleven for coffee. Among the coffees offered at the self-serve beverage bar was a Brazilian dark roast. Rocket fuel for the morning's writing. A sign on the door featured an offer of coffee and a donut for two dollars. I didn't take them up on the donut, but got the coffee for a dollar. A good deal, considering what I'd pay at any of the upscale coffee shops in the area.

On subsequent days, I found myself waiting in a line of shoppers balancing their coffee/donut combo along with other assorted items. The woman behind the counter was always the same, and after a few days she recognized me, and when she saw me with my filled coffee mug she would put out her hand to receive my dollar bill so I could leave without waiting in line.

One morning I was late getting my day underway, and it was ten a.m. before I got to the 7-Eleven. It was a Sunday, and I expected to see a different face behind the counter, but it was the same woman. There was no one waiting at the checkout counter when I walked in, so I stopped before going to the beverage bar.

"Don't you get a day off?" I asked.

She shook her head and smiled. "Every day the same," she said.

I got my coffee, came back to the counter, and handed her my dollar bill. "You make much better coffee than I do," I told her.

She was laughing as I left.

Although they may seem insignificant, such events represent the healing salve we have the opportunity to apply to the world every time we step into it, a barely perceptible ripple set in motion across a sea of separation and loneliness.

What He Did for Me

It's a cold and drizzly downcast day, and I'm running late for an appointment. I get into my car and notice the fuel gauge is on empty. Berating myself for having neglected to fill the tank the last time I was out, I stop at the first gas station I come to and walk into the station to prepay for fuel.

A bright-faced young man behind the counter greets me with a smile. "What can I do for you?" he asks in a cheery voice that counteracts both my mood and the sodden weather.

Choice point: Do I allow the dark mood I entered with to prevail and stay in my private world of self-recrimination and victimhood? Or say yes to the offer of a friendly connection?

"Ten on pump eleven," I say, matching his bright tone as I hand him a twenty-dollar bill with a return smile.

Another, even brighter, smile from this young, unwitting healer. “You got it!” he says, as he hands me my change.

I leave uplifted by real contact with a fellow human who invited me into relationship, however brief. He changed the course of my day by modeling what I, in turn, offered others as I went on to my appointment in a transformed state of mind.

Living Legacy

A few years ago Richard and I discovered that green burials are available at a funeral facility only ten miles from where we live. We recently made a long-postponed trip to begin the process of prearranging our “final address” after a life moving about the country.

On our way home, we stopped at a supermarket to pick up a few groceries. I grabbed a small cart and began walking toward the grocery aisles, passing a young mother with a baby in the cart’s child seat and a small girl of four or five walking beside her. The little girl stepped in front of Richard, who was a few steps behind me, causing him to step aside to avoid bumping into her. I turned when I heard the mother apologizing.

Richard was smiling at her and asked where she had found them, gesturing toward the two children.

The mother looked puzzled.

“In what aisle?” Richard clarified.

Getting the joke, the mother joined the fun.

“Aisle seventeen,” she said.

“Ah,” Richard replied, “but you’ve already gotten the best ones.”

Who knows how much longer any of us will grace the earth in living bodies? While we're here, why not leave smiles on the faces of those we encounter?

Winter Wonder

It's been a long week of short days and drizzle. A tough December. As I arise on yet another cold, wet day, I decide to make an early trip to the market to get the makings for a big pot of chili to offset the chilly weather. Comfort food.

It's still dark when I've finished my breakfast. The winter sun rises slowly and reluctantly in the Northwest, even on the rare clear day, but this particular morning it's raining—hard. Putting in some writing time seems more appealing than venturing out in the dark and rain, so I choose to postpone the shopping trip and instead sit down at the computer with a mug of hot tea.

Two hours later, the rain has almost stopped. Feeling good about the writing I've produced, I gather my cloth grocery bags—a nod to developing relationship with the earth and its gifts—and drive to the supermarket.

Ten minutes later, when I pull into the parking lot, the sun has sent the gray clouds scuttling and is poking its way through fluffy white cloud pillows polka-dotting an azure blue sky. As I park and get out of the car, I'm greeted by a rainbow of breathtaking intensity stretching east to west over the city, a gift from the sky gods.

Heading for the store entrance, I encounter an elderly woman, her head down, hunched over an empty shopping cart which she's pushing toward the return cart enclosure.

"Look," I say, pointing upward. She lifts her head, and her upturned face lights up, wonder replacing dejection as she gasps with delight. Other customers leaving the store, intent on whatever was occupying their inner lives, see us and raise their faces to the rainbow. Smiles replace complacency. Faces become alive. Mouths remark on the wonder of it all. Fingers point as others leave the store.

For a brief moment, *me* has become *we*, and bright relationship burns away the gray clouds of separation.

Receiving a RAK

When I first discovered the website *randomactsofkindness.org* it was in conjunction with an assignment chosen by a writing group I participated in several years ago. It was prior to the inspiration to write this book, so planning to intentionally go into the world and offer a kindness was a challenge I hadn't yet envisioned.

The assignment was to pick a suggestion from those listed on the RAK site, perform the action, and write about it. I expected picking something would be easy, but there were so many options I had trouble deciding among them.

While I was contemplating the exhaustive list of possibilities, a thought occurred to me. Rather than pick a specific action in advance, why not just go into the real world with the intention to be alert for opportunities to offer small kindnesses in whatever situation I found myself?

I set off the next morning for the supermarket, congratulating myself on my insight and intention. Releasing a shopping cart from the queue, I started my routine course through the store, shopping list in hand—and routinely went into my internally focused, task-oriented safe space.

It wasn't until I was in the parking lot transferring several overloaded shopping bags from the cart to my trunk that I woke up and realized my good intentions hadn't made it through my first stop in the produce department.

My car was parked on a slope sufficient to require keeping one foot on the cart as I unloaded it to prevent it from escaping. As I was placing the last of the bags into the trunk, a gentleman of my own generation put a hand on the cart and said, "Let me take that for you." We proceeded to have a pleasant interchange about the hazards of runaway shopping carts, and I turned out to be the recipient rather than the provider of a random act of kindness.

To Market, to Market

The downtown Saturday farmers market opens at ten a.m. I usually get there early to get a parking spot in a nearby lot that charges during the week but not on weekends. Unfortunately, the sign giving rates and instructions for how to pay doesn't make clear that the rates are in effect Monday through Friday only. This is a problem for people unfamiliar with the lot.

Bellingham gets a lot of summer tourists, and when I arrive there is almost always someone—often several someones—standing beneath the sign, credit card in hand, trying to figure out how to pay. Before I head for the market a block away, I make a stop to tell the befuddled shopper(s) that Saturdays are free. The response is always a degree of gratitude more appropriate to having handed the person a winning lottery ticket than to saving them a parking fee. Sometimes I think I should just bring a folding chair and a book and spend Saturday mornings sitting next to the parking sign, freeing shoppers from the anxiety of not being able to figure out how to pay but not wanting to go off without paying and getting a parking ticket.

Typically, after garnering thanks from puzzled parkers, I enter the market in high spirits, which are quickly deflated when I'm confronted by dozens of displays of local produce and products ranging from T-shirts and pottery to high-end jewelry and clothing. The merchants sit beside their wares keeping an eye out for prospective customers. I'm reluctant to stop or even to make eye contact and offer a smile or greeting if I'm not planning on buying anything, and I most often find myself proceeding along the aisles to the bread stand, the produce peddler, or the egg lady with eyes straight ahead, focused on what I'm there to buy.

It's a perfect example of allowing a story (If I stop to look and don't buy anything I'll offend the vendor) to co-opt my attention and create anxiety and self-consciousness. The result is that I've taken my attention offline and I'm not present to opportunities for connection and service.

Such was the case when one morning I stopped at a booth to get coffee. I ordered a medium cup. The price was $2.25. I handed the young woman behind the counter two one-dollar bills and what I thought was a quarter but was actually a nickel. When she brought it to my attention, I gave her a third dollar instead. As she handed me my change, she smiled and said, "Now you have three quarters."

As I stepped aside to put the change in my wallet, the woman who had been behind me in line took my place and asked if she could get a smaller cup since she had only two dollars. It wasn't until I'd pocketed my three quarters and walked away that it occurred to me that if I'd been present in the space instead of stuck in my head, I would have taken one of my three quarters and offered it to her so she could get the larger cup of coffee.

What happens next when opportunities such as this are missed is crucial. Do I add another brick to the negative story I've built about myself? (I am the person who is so self-involved I'm not present to make connections and be of service.) Or live and learn so I'm better prepared for the next opportunity?

Timing Is Everything

I've put off doing laundry until we're down to the last set of clean sheets and towels. My intention is to hit the laundry facility early, but one thing leads to another (don't they always?), and by the time I get to the laundry room it's late afternoon. As I begin loading my clothes into two large washers, another woman comes in with a heavy load, puts it down, and stands quietly looking at the machines. I wonder if she's having difficulty figuring out how to use them.

Choice point: Do I mind my own business and silently leave? Or risk offering unneeded assistance and take the chance of having her regard me as intrusive, or perhaps even insulting by assuming she can't do her own laundry?

"Excuse me," I say, as I approach her. She looks up at me. "Could you use some help?" I ask.

Her acceptance of my offer is immediate, delivered with a grateful smile. She tells me she's a caretaker at a local retirement home and usually does her wash at work. I show her how to operate the machines, explaining that they're new, and adding that I had trouble figuring out how they worked the first time I used them.

Rather than rush off, I pause long enough to give her a chance to talk. She tells me about her mother, who has had a stroke, and how she and her sister are sharing their mother's care so she can stay in her own home.

When I leave, we exchange first names and she thanks me again for my assistance.

Had I done my laundry in the morning, as I'd planned, I wouldn't have been available to render a kindness to this neighbor. The thought leaves me pondering the possibility that when we've made a commitment to serve, some form of cosmic intelligence puts us where service is needed.

Piercing the Curtain

It's a quiet weekday morning when I stop at a local chain drugstore to pick up some mailing supplies. The store aisles are mostly empty.

When I get to the checkout area, there's a line. As I take my place behind the man ahead of me, he turns and brandishes a copper-coated sauté pan.

"Have you ever used one of these things?" he asks, his eyes twinkling and his tone playful. I tell him I've seen them advertised on TV but haven't bought one.

"I'm a sucker for TV ads," he volunteers, and proceeds to engage me in a lively conversation peppered with questions like whether I think the pan really contains the titanium boldly advertised on the cardboard packaging.

In the meantime, another man has joined the line, and then another woman. All of us are drawn into the impromptu conversation initiated by the sauté-pan man.

Such people are a ray of sunshine piercing the gray curtain of isolation that so many of us hide behind when we go into a world of strangers. How ironic that we so often stand just inches away from each other physically while inhabiting an inner world that's a universe away. Being present and available when opportunities for a brief engagement such as this one arise allows us to step through the curtain and join the party.

Meeting Sam

It was the kind of fall day that begged for a walk. Brisk but sunny after a week of heavy clouds and drizzle. I put on my walking shoes and headed for the trail that borders the west side of the apartment complex.

As I stepped from the sidewalk onto the wooded trail, I saw laboring toward me a middle-aged woman with both arms stretched downward by large, overloaded grocery bags. Under one arm she was clutching a bulk package of paper towels.

As I approached her, I slowed and remarked, "You've got more than a full load there." She looked up and acknowledged my observation with a smile and a nod.

"Can I help you carry them?" I asked. It didn't require thought. It was just the appropriate response in that moment. Her smile grew bigger as she said, with a tone that registered both surprise and gratitude, "Would you mind?"

I took one of the bags and the paper towels and turned around, following her back into the apartment complex and to her unit.

Thus I met Sam. Although we were strangers to one another, my simple offer of help that was clearly needed created an instant bond. We chatted as we walked to her unit, and when we got there I discovered that Sam is an artist. Her nature paintings were propped against the sofa, the dining table, and along the walls, bringing the Northwest woods inside. We continued chatting and laughing, sharing information about ourselves and our lives, for twenty or thirty minutes before I left to resume my walk.

I haven't encountered Sam since, but for a brief moment in time we impacted each other's lives in a gesture of neighborly friendship offered and received.

And Then There Is John

It's after dinner on an early summer evening, and as I prepare to make granola for the next day's breakfast I realize we're out of oats. I put on my walking shoes and hit the trail for a short walk to the local market. When I get there, I go to the bulk food section, bag the oats, pick up a few bananas, and head for the checkout stands.

The store is sparsely populated on a lush and lazy Sunday evening, and there are only two lanes open. A customer is being checked out in one of them. John, a checker I haven't seen before, is waiting behind the counter of the second, which is empty.

Apparently, he's been waiting for me. At least that's the impression I get, because the smile he graces me with as I put my purchases on the counter makes me feel like a long-lost beloved relative. No kidding! This young man, surely no older than twenty, has the rotund face and body of a miniature Santa Claus—minus the beard. If I was five and he was sitting in an overstuffed chair, I'd climb into his lap.

Any trace of social anxiety I might still harbor melts in the warmth of his thousand-watt smile as he greets me. When I remark on what a happy person he appears to be, he says, turning the smile wattage even higher, "It's a gorgeous day. I'm above ground. What more could I want?"

Indeed! Although I haven't seen him since, just knowing John is somewhere in the world beaming his smile like a lighthouse in a dark sea makes me happy.

Creating We

On a balmy spring evening bathed in the floral fragrance of budding lilacs, I enter the street-level meeting space of our local library. The occasion is the monthly meeting of the local chapter of the Institute of Noetic Sciences. I don't attend regularly, but the topic for this one caught my attention: Who Are You Becoming?

When I enter the space, there are perhaps fifteen people—none of whom I know—sitting in folding chairs aligned in tidy rows facing a podium, or standing and chatting with others. True to my introvert nature, I find a seat several rows from the front in an unoccupied section, settle myself, notebook in hand, and await the start of the meeting.

Within several minutes the number of people in the room has doubled, and the main presenter, one of a group of six, stands behind the podium and explains what we're there for. To my surprise, it turns out it's to be an experiential evening. She explains that we'll be meeting in small groups of six or seven, plus one member of the presenting team. We'll each be given a sheet of paper with three questions written across the top and spaces below each question for three rounds of answers. Beginning with the presenting team member, each person in the group will address the person to his or her left by name, and ask, in order, each of the three questions at the top of the sheet.

1. What is one thing I can do to explore and expand my co-creative consciousness?
2. What effect would this have on me personally?
3. What effect would this have on my community?

The person sitting opposite the one answering the questions is to record on the handout sheet a brief summary of what was said.

Imagine yourself having arrived at a meeting with chairs arranged in rows facing a podium, expecting a traditional presentation on the announced topic, requiring nothing more of the audience than polite attention, and offering in return the right to remain silent. Then imagine being enrolled in a participatory event where anonymity isn't an option.

Such is my situation on this gentle spring evening—I who court invisibility and virtually never speak in public events of any kind.

After much shuffling of chairs, I find myself in a circle with seven other people, none of whom know one another. The team leader introduces herself by name (I promptly forget it in my mounting anxiety), and we go around the circle giving our first names.

The first round is a bit tense and awkward. The second person questioned is the one whose answers I'm supposed to record, but I'm so busy thinking about what I'm going to say when I'm questioned—and realizing in horror that I've forgotten the name of the woman to my left, whom *I'm* supposed to question—that I forget to listen to, much less record, the answers of the man sitting across from me.

And so it goes around the circle as we settle into this exercise we've somehow found ourselves shanghaied into.

By the second round, we've remembered each other's names and to record the response of the person opposite us, and everyone seems to be breathing a bit easier. A group relaxation is occurring. There's even a bit of tentative humor.

By the third round, we're comrades-in-arms, kindred souls, smiling and laughing.

At the end of the third round, we're instructed to discuss among ourselves and then list the general categories into which our responses to the first question fell, then to appoint a spokesperson to report to the larger group.

When we all come back together—moving our chairs not into the neat rows we began the evening with but quite haphazardly, in some spontaneously organic fashion—it's as if the room has been bathed in sunlight. I'm not a person who "reads" energy, but the whole room feels elevated and enlivened. As each spokesperson offers their group's most common responses to the question "What is one thing I can do to explore and expand my co-creative consciousness?" it becomes clear that, although there is a great overlapping of responses, each group has developed a distinct personality, and a group bonding has occurred.

After all the groups have reported, with much laughter and banter, people begin offering comments about their personal experience and impressions of the exercise we've all engaged in over the past hour.

The most poignant and moving is "We discovered *we*."

I leave pondering the question that drew me to the meeting—Who am I becoming?—from a new perspective, and wonder whether my day-to-day life choices are defending my shy, retiring, insular *me*, or moving me toward creating *we* wherever I find myself.

Who are you becoming?

ISN'T IT AMAZING?

I was sitting with Richard at the kitchen table. We had just finished lunch: leftover vegetable bean soup I'd made the evening before and a fresh loaf of crusty artisan bread that I'd picked up that morning at a local bakery. After he took his last bite, he put down his soup spoon, folded his napkin, and said, "You're amazing."

Without missing a beat, I replied, uncharacteristically, "I know," followed by, "Aren't we all?"

This simple five-second interchange left me thinking about how often I overlook such everyday opportunities for connection—an interchange that would probably go unnoticed by anyone listening in. Why is it so hard for us to perceive and acknowledge that we are all, indeed, amazing? How would it change the world we live in—the one within and the one without— if we did?

Take your amazing self into the world with a smile and a light heart, and it will be reflected back to you. Be the change you want to see.

The world is waiting for you.

EPILOGUE

Three things in human life are important: the first is to be kind; the second is to be kind; and the third is to be kind.

—Henry James

So here we are, back where we began, with Henry James's observation and prescription for what is important in life. If you're still with me, I know for sure that you're a kindred soul. And we have work to do together. Wherever you are, whoever you are—introvert, extrovert, or somewhere in between—you've heard the call, and you know what needs to be done. It may not be writing a book or starting a movement, but whatever it is, know that you're not alone.

Never doubt your ability to make a difference in a world that badly needs kind souls who are willing to offer smiles in whatever form we're moved to deliver them. If that means pushing against your comfort envelope, have faith that you can do it.

When I began writing in January of 2017, I couldn't imagine the person I see now when I look in the mirror. The person who can experience delight instead of dread when she approaches a stranger at a checkout stand or in the boarding line at the airport gate, or the family with a child in a stroller and a dog trotting beside them on the trail. The person who can speak in public for a cause she truly believes in. The transformation has happened in small but consistent increments, one encounter at a time. It hasn't always been easy. It still isn't. But people don't scare me so much anymore. And even if it they do, I know I can handle it.

So can you.

How wonderful it is that nobody need wait a single moment before starting to improve the world.

—Anne Frank

ACKNOWLEDGMENTS

My deepest gratitude . . .

To Richard, life partner and life coach, who began asking "When are you going to write your book?" decades ago.

To Rick and Jeff, not only for their love and support as beloved sons, but for their expertise and contribution in all things technological. You wouldn't be reading this book without them.

To my daughters-in-law, Clelia Lewis and Terri van der Vlugt, and to my grandchildren: Nate, Ruby, Rhys, Seren, and Aditya. Kind souls all—who give me the motivation to persist in my efforts to make the world a kinder, more inclusive place for them and for future generations.

To the WE Squad—Gloria Harrison, Ham Hayes, Skye Burn, Deborah Moskowitz, and Richard Lewis (Yes, THAT Richard)—who have been with me every step of the way: prodding, encouraging, coaching, supporting in more ways than I can count, including not accepting my reluctance to do the thing I thought I could not do.

To my many test readers over the years this book has been in progress for their support, encouragement, and feedback that kept me on track and focused on my mission.

To all the strangers I've smiled at and acknowledged and who have responded in kind, giving me the courage to persist in this late-life mission. They have provided the stories that flesh out my observations and reflections on the nature of being human.

To my readers: May you pay kindness forward, even if you're scared.

To Lee. For it all.

I cannot emphasize enough: be kind, be generous, be forbearing, be forgiving, be gentle, be understanding, be accepting, be tender-hearted . . . I cannot plead this case enough, I cannot in any way trivialize these wishes, so please: be kind, be generous, be forbearing, be forgiving, be understanding, be accepting, be tender-hearted.

—Lee Lozowick

Nov. 18, 1943 – Nov. 16, 2010

ABOUT THE AUTHOR

The seed that became *Smiling at Strangers* was planted in 1955, when Nancy Lewis received a surprise award for Excellence in English at the Senior Awards Ceremony of her high school in New London, Connecticut. Nancy remembers telling her mother the next morning, "Someday I'm going to write a book. But first I have to get some life experience." Six decades of life experience later, at the age of 80, she began to write that book. The intervening "experience" has included marriage to a life partner; two sons and five grandchildren; college and university degrees; employment as an English teacher, librarian, and freelance editor; and residence in six states plus British Columbia. She currently lives with her husband Richard in Bellingham, Washington, where she continues to look for opportunities to offer smiles and small kindnesses to strangers. For further information see her website at www.smilingatstrangers.net.